C000213112

# JEWISH EXILE IN INDIA
1933-1945

# JEWISH EXILE IN INDIA

## 1933-1945

*Edited by*

ANIL BHATTI
JOHANNES H. VOIGT

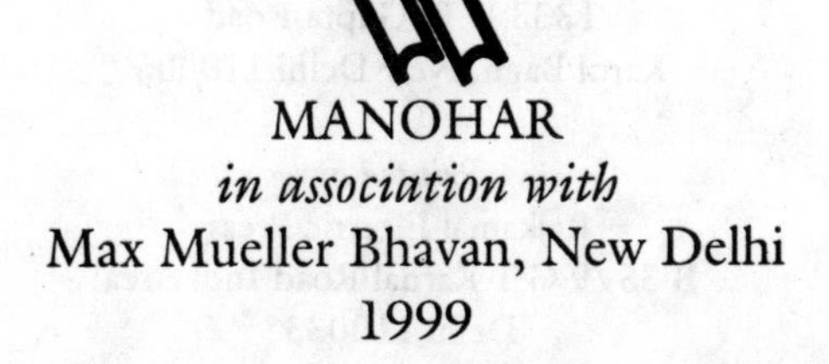

MANOHAR
*in association with*
Max Mueller Bhavan, New Delhi
1999

First published 1999



ISBN 81-7304-237-3

*Published by*
Ajay Kumar Jain for
Manohar Publishers & Distributors
2/6 Ansari Road, Daryaganj
New Delhi 110002

*Typeset by*
A J Software Publishing Co. Pvt. Ltd.
305 Durga Chambers
1333 D.B. Gupta Road
Karol Bagh, New Delhi 110005

*Printed at*
Rajkamal Electric Press
B 35/9 G T Karnal Road Indl Area
Delhi 110033

# Contents

RECEPTIONS AND REFLECTIONS

# Illustrations

# ILLUSTRATIONS

# Preface

Half a century was to pass since the end of the Second World War and the defeat of Nazism in Germany and Europe before India as a haven for the persecuted Jews from 1933 to 1945 was taken up as a subject of a coordinated effort of research. Although a considerable amount of international research on exile and emigration had been carried out in the 1970s and 1980s, and although the importance of Shanghai as a desired place of refuge by boat via Indian ports was known, almost no scholarly effort had been directed towards India. The publication of an essay on Jewish emigration to India (in *Wechselwirkungen*, Yearbook of Stuttgart University of 1991) indicated the manifold aspects of emigration to India. It needed, however, another effort, a combined one to bring to light the fate of those who escaped the holocaust, and to elucidate their work and fate in the political, social and cultural environment in India.

The symposium held at the Centre of German Studies, Jawaharlal Nehru University, on 15 and 16 March 1995, was the result of such an endeavour, and in keeping with the complexity of the subject the participants were scholars from the various fields of history, social sciences and literary criticism. Together with the emphasis on the necessity of interdisciplinary research, the contemporary relevance of the subject was highlighted by the fact that the Ambassadors of the Federal Republic of Germany and Israel and the Chargé d'Affaires of Austria were among the speakers during the inauguration.

The papers presented at the symposium and a few additional ones make up the three parts of this book. The first part deals with British-Indian and Indian policies and Jewish and Indian responses, the second contains contributions to the work and achievements of some well-known Jewish émigrés, and the third part consists of analyses and descriptions of literary works and reminiscences on the situation of Jewish refugees in India.

This book owes its publication first of all to the work, patience and confidence of the authors of the contributions. But for the help of a number of organizations and colleagues neither the symposium nor this publication would have been possible. We would like to record our gratitude to the Max Mueller Bhavan and the office of the German Academic Exchange Service in New Delhi, and the Jawaharlal Nehru University. We would like to thank especially Georg Lechner and Tilmann Waldraff, former and present directors of the Max Mueller Bhavan, New Delhi, and Manfred Stassen, director of the New Delhi office of the German Academic Exchange Service for their support. We are grateful to Rekha Kamath from the Centre of German Studies and Petra Matusche from the Max Mueller Bhavan for their help. The symposium was enriched by an exhibition of drawings by Rudolf von Leyden and by Situ Singh Buehler's and Justin McCarthy's performance of compositions by Walter Kaufmann. Our thanks go to Anna Winterberg from the Max Mueller Bhavan, Bombay, and to H. Goebel-Gross respectively for organizing the artistic complement to the symposium. To all of those who assisted in organizing the symposium, we owe our thanks.

The best we can hope for is that this book may stimulate further research in a subject nearly forgotten, yet still important for the fields of Indian and German studies.

ANIL BHATTI (New Delhi)
JOHANNES H. VOIGT (Stuttgart)

# INTRODUCTORY

# Persecution of the Jewish People: Prelude to the Holocaust

*Johannes H. Voigt*

When the people belonging to Jewish faith were emancipated, they stood to benefit in that they received the full citizenship of the respective German states of which they were resident. This significant development took place in the first half of the nineteenth century. Consequently an unprecedented upsurge in Jewish activities was witnessed. These activities in turn led to many noteworthy achievements in virtually all spheres of social life. For instance, in the economic sphere, Jewish activities coincided with Germany's industrialization. In the political sphere, these activities supported Germany's bid for unity and search for liberty. In the academic sphere, these activities resulted in epoch making scientific accomplishments. Finally, in the literary and philosophical spheres these activities transformed Germany into a much admired centre of culture and education.

An important point to be noted is that the Jewish contribution to German society and by extension to its culture went far beyond the proportion of the population of this community (such contribution was made over a century beginning in the early nineteenth century). The Jews constituted only 1 per cent of the total German population. The Jewish achievements were indistinguishable from the overall German resurgence as most of the Jewish people claimed and they really were assimilated or integrated as members of the German nation. Despite such patriotism among the Jews, there were lingering remnants of anti-Semitism whose origins lay in the Middle Ages and can be attributed to Christian church. Such anti-Semitism took on dangerous political overtones, especially among those strata of society which believed in fostering racial hatred.

The volatile amalgam of ideas and ideologies born out of envy towards the Jews, social Darwinism and traditional Christian anti-

Semitism, was carried right into the early part of the twentieth century, new 'ingredients' were added to this amalgam after the end of the First World War.

It was at this critical point of time that the cliques responsible for leading Germany to defeat and subsequent disaster were searching for convenient excuses and culprits to pin the blame on. The 'stab in the back' legend, and the 'Jewish conspiracy' thesis were proferred as common explanations in military and right-wing circles. Adolf Hitler, in his search for a nationalistic ideology, drew largely from such an amalgam of fabricated legends, prejudices and conspiratorial theories.

And while Germany was falling victim to legends and was coming under the spell of Hitler's nationalistic and militaristic movement, India came under the spell of Mahatma Gandhi and was following his leadership in a non-violent struggle for independence. The political courses of the two nations in the 1930s were entirely in opposite directions. Whereas Germany set out to rearm itself and conquer, India was avoiding an armed conflagration with the British by agreeing to moderate constitutional reforms in 1935, which envisaged provincial autonomy, though withheld decisive political influence at the centre. The German nation, on the other hand, let itself be deprived of constitutional rights to accept the shackles of an unprecedented system of tyranny. The contrast of political ideals and activities in India and Germany could not have been greater: in the former the Mahatma struggled peacefully for justice and freedom and in the latter the 'Fuehrer' subdued all opposition by force and determined to conquer new territories. In India, the effort was to pull down all artificial and traditional social barriers between human beings and in Germany new barriers of race, faith and nationality were being raised. The Hindu endorsed Christ's Sermon on the Mount, the other, nominally a Christian, disseminating hatred and violence amongst mankind.

To all those who wanted to read and were patient enough to make their way through hundreds of pages written in a clumsy, complicated style, and were able to stand pseudo-historical legends and lies and a considerable amount of vitriolic hatred, Hitler's book *Mein Kampf*, written during his year of confinement in a fortress and published in the mid-1920s, made perfectly clear the course of politics to be expected if he were to get at the helm of affairs in Germany. Hitler envisaged huge expansion of the Reich towards the East for the sake of 'living' space. It was obvious that such a goal was attainable only by war. His second aim was announced in equally unmistakable terms: a war on Jews aiming at their removal from German territory by all means available.[1]

Once in power Hitler never abandoned his final goals, despite his denials. In conversation with Indians and others, he emphasized that his ideas in *Mein Kampf* were not to be taken literally. He called it a book written in political circumstances long since passed.[2] Hitler approached his goals cautiously, making sure that he was treading on safe ground and that no internal or external opposition would block the way towards German expansion and Jewish extermination.

As Chancellor of the Reich, Hitler used a whole arsenal of multifarious weapons for action against the Jewish people in Germany, reaching from personal victimization by incarceration in concentration camps to ostracism of entire professional groups such as administrators, bankers, merchants, medical doctors, scientists and artists; from individual discrimination and deprivation to boycott of shops and firms; from physical terror to nation-wide pogroms; from discriminatory laws to special anti-Jewish legislation, like the Nuremberg laws, defining who was to be regarded a 'Jew' and who an 'Aryan', thus establishing apartheid in Germany.[3] Foreign economic pressure on Germany like that of the Tata Iron and Steel Company, came far too late and did not have any impact on Nazi policy.[4] Also Gandhi supported a policy of boycott against Germany: 'boycott foreign goods, not foreign ability. And I feel keenly for the persecuted Jews'.[5]

In the first half of Hitler's 12-year rule, Nazi policy was aimed at forcing the Jews to emigrate, regardless of the merits in their service to society and the nation. And tens of thousands did emigrate, their major problem being: whereto? The USA did not open its gates more than it was obliged to on account of the quota system of immigration fixed in the 1920s. Britain was allowing thousands to stay temporarily, hoping that the migrants would find a place to live in her overseas empire or elsewhere. But few of the colonial governments felt obliged to open their gates. British India raised its barrier of entry in early 1938, either because of fear that it would be burdened with meeting the expense for people stranded there or because of protests from various sections of the Indian society against the immigration of European Jews.

Viceroy Linlithgow was extremely reluctant to lift British India's barriers for the entry of Jewish refugees. He answered an appeal to this effect by the British Government in May 1938 in a telegram:

> While recognising desirability on humanitarian grounds of helping Jewish refugees I feel that, in view of the difficulties in the way of foreigners from Western countries finding employment in India, it would be prudent to admit only such Jewish refugees as are found after careful investigation, to be not politically undesirable and to have friends in India responsible for their support.[6]

The stand-off attitude of most of the nations was reflected in the deliberations and resolutions of the conference at Évian situated on the French-Swiss border in July 1938. In this conference, delegates from thirty-two states were summoned at the request of the American President Franklin Delano Roosevelt in order to help German Jewish refugees with concrete immigration and settlement proposals. British India did not participate in this conference though invited as a member of the League of Nations. The outcome was anything but encouraging for the desperate Jewish refugees and Jews in Germany still waiting for the possibility and permission to emigrate to a place of safety. No additional openings were found. The USA stuck to its combined quota of German and Austrian immigrants, viz., 27,000 persons per annum. The only country to oblige was Australia which belatedly agreed to offer refuge to 15,000 persons at the rate of 5000 per annum, of which only this number of the first batch was to arrive until the outbreak of War in 1939 when the shipping stopped. The setting up of the Inter-Governmental Committee (IGC) was to take the refugee question—and with it international complaints about German terror against the Jews—out of high-power politics, and thus free the foreign offices from squabbling with German authorities over financial questions, as these had turned out to be the most pressing ones. The IGC negotiated from December 1938 till the beginning of the Second World War with German authorities about the terms on which German Jews were to leave their country, but achieved only limited success.

The logical question would be: Why was so very little achieved? The official efforts to help were largely half-hearted. Hitler's words and deeds were not taken at their face value. British India was no exception to the rule. In such circumstances, Gandhi's appeals and Nehru's warnings were 'merely voices in the wilderness'.[7]

It is obvious that the appeasing tendency which characterized the foreign policies of the Western European powers towards Hitler's aggressiveness and greed had also a moderating affect on their policies towards the anti-Jewish persecution in Germany. Prime Minister Sir

Neville Chamberlain's accommodating spirit in Munich allowing Germany to occupy the Sudeten territory of Czechoslovakia, was accompanied by an acquiescence with regard to the terror unleashed earlier after the *Anschluss* of Austria and later by the nationwide pogrom of 9/10 November 1938, the so-called *Reichskristallnacht*. The fear of endangering the policy of appeasement along with the self-consoling justification that the terror might become worse if it were exposed and criticized by foreign governments, the British and other countries' foreign offices refrained from calling a spade a spade. The Jewish imbroglio was forcibly looked upon as an internal German problem, though, in effect, it was having its repercussions in all corners of the world. It was, moreover, a massive violation of human rights, of which all the world knew about but officially kept quiet. Thus, 'appeasement' was also the line pursued in confrontation with Nazi Germany's racial terrorism.

Many of the persecuted Jews, who had a chance, abandoned their homes, families, friends, places of work and all that was dear to them, and chose to live in exile in order to escape further victimization. They sought accceptance in many countries, including British India. Nearly all of them were destitutes, who could offer nothing but their skills and gifts and goodwill. In the end such qualities benefited the countries which had opened their gates to them, including India. They left the marks of their contribution in many fields of activity.

In his speech on 30 January 1939, i.e. seven months before the German onslaught on Poland, Hitler gave a clear warning of what would happen to the Jewish people of Europe in case of war. 'Let me be a prophet again today: if the international clique of Jewish High Finance within Europe and without should be able to drag the nations again into a world war, then its result will not be the Bolshevisation of the earth and thus the victory of Judaism but the destruction of the Jewish race in Europe.'[8]

The search for an appropriate place for settling hundreds of thousands of Jewish migrants kept the IGC busy in 1938-9, with Guiana in South America as a possible choice, but ill-suited both climatically and financially. After the collapse of France in mid-1940, German authorities were fixing their eyes again on the East African island of Madagascar, envisaged by the Nazis ever since 1938 as a possible settlement colony for German Jews. Though all plans concerning it as a refuge were found Utopian, Hitler kept on talking about it, long after he had found another answer to the Jewish question: its 'final solution'.

With the outbreak of the Second World War an unprecedented forcible migration of people was inaugurated. Poles were shifted towards the east, ethnic Germans towards the west, and Jewish people were concentrated in ghettos and reserved areas in order to control and lay hold on them whenever the order was given. Before the year 1939 came to an end, the first batch of German Jews had been deported into Jewish ghettos in Poland. The administrative machinery of the Gestapo and the S.S. under Heinrich Himmler and his second-in-command, Reinhard Heydrich, was preparing for a deportation of nearly three million Jewish people and at the same time camouflaging its activities during the course of 1940 by still referring to 'Madagascar' as the possible destination, but in reality having in mind only annihilation.

Another fateful step with regard to the Jews was taken in consequence of the war against the USSR, termed by the Nazis as a war of ideologies. An order to exterminate all Jewish officers in the Soviet army had been prepared months before the attack. It was interpreted as a command to exterminate indiscriminately all prisoners and civil authorities for political and racist reasons.

In connection with the German invasion of the Soviet Union, the decision for reaching a 'final solution' was taken. An announcement indicated a turn for the worse: the stoppage of all emigration from Germany and German-occupied territories in October 1941. Meanwhile, the so-called *Einsatzgruppen* (operational squads) had begun mass shootings behind the frontline. When the planners and organizers discovered that this was not the most effective way to achieve the goal of the 'final solution', another method tried earlier in a programme of eugenic killing people with mental disorders by gas poisoning, was chosen as a 'more efficient' and more secretive means. On 20 January 1942, at the so-called 'Wannsee Conference', Reinhard Heydrich, in charge of the 'final solution', explained to senior administrators of all governmental departments concerned, the general framework of the programme. Although the protocol referred verbally to 'liquidation by labour', there was no mincing of words during the briefing and the ensuing discussion. Everybody present knew what was implied, as explained later by Adolf Eichmann in his trial: 'killing, elimination and annihilation'.

For the purpose of extermination, huge camps were constructed, the largest and the most notorious being Auschwitz. The task was to exterminate Jews and other 'enemies' either by overworking them or killing them in gas chambers. In early 1942, the machinery for mass extermination was set in motion. Millions of Jews from all corners of German and German-occupied or dominated Europe were transported by railway to the extermination camps. It was only the reconquest of the territory by Soviet forces which brought to an end this extermination process which was unprecedented in history.

The number of Jews killed during the Nazi regime varies between five and six million. This figure includes men, women and children. Those of the Jewish people in Europe who escaped the mass murder owed their life to luck and the refuge found in other nations including India. On the Indian subcontinent approximately a thousand Jewish refugees found a place for survival.

There was hardly anybody in Germany and elsewhere who, before the Second World War, could imagine what would happen eventually—the holocaust. Most of the Germans and foreign statesmen seem to have turned a deaf ear towards and a blind eye to obvious writings on the wall. Even Gandhi, realizing the viciousness of the German anti-Jewish terror and professing that if a war were justified for any reason, it would be a war against Germany on account of the inhuman treatment of her Jewish citizens, could not imagine the immensity of the barbarism which was to follow. His advice that German Jews resort to non-violent means of opposition, as he himself had practised it against racism in South Africa and in India in her struggle for freedom, was completely out of place. Neither he nor most foreigners comprehended that British rule in India and Hitler's rule in Germany were worlds apart, politically and morally. Hitler's ideal of the British Raj was as wrong as Gandhi's ideas of the Nazi system.

Hitler and his followers had hoped that none of their barbaric doings would ever come to light. They were mistaken; sufficient witnesses survived to tell their story of hell on earth. Many of the henchmen put to trial confesssed and described in detail the working of their killing machinery. And last but not the least, huge masses of documents have survived and enable historians to get a more vivid picture of how the system worked, which not even the most imaginative mind could have invented.

Many historians are still working to find out more facts, facets and details of the persecution, the holocaust and the consequences of exile. The fate of the Jewish people in exile has only been partly explored. A lot of research work will have to be done by historians in the respective countries all over the world, including India. This task needs the experience of scholars in various disciplines. The story of the Jewish exile in India will form part of Jewish, Indian, British and German history.

## NOTES

1. The interconnection betwen expansion in the East and removal of the Jews from Germany and occupied territory in Hitler's amalgam of ideas has been convincingly analysed and explained by Eberhard Jäckel, *Hitler's Weltanschaung*, Stuttgart: DVA, 1981.
2. On Hitler's interview with Dr A.L. Sinha on 6 December 1935, see Johannes H. Voigt, 'Hitler und Indien', in *Vierteljahrshefte für Zeitgeschichte*, 1971, No.1, pp. 33-63, esp. pp. 45ff. On Hitler's meeting with Subhas Chandra Bose, see Johannes H. Voigt, *India in the Second World War*, New Delhi: Arnold-Heinemann, 1987, p. 137.
3. The term 'Aryan' used in official Nazi terminology implied something quite different from the Indian terminology; it meant in Germany then simply 'non-Jewish'.
4. On Indian examples of boycott see Milan Hauner, *India in Axis' Strateqy*, Stuttgart: 1981, p. 76.
5. *Collected Works of Mahatma Gandhi*, Ahmedabad: 1976, Vol. 76, p. 298.
6. Viceroy to the Secretary of State for India, Tel. 737-S, 31 May 1938, India Office Library Records. L/P&J/8/750.
7. On Gandhi and Nehru's attitudes see Johannes H. Voigt, 'Die Emigration von Juden aus Mitteleuropa nach Indian während der Verfolgung durch das NS-Regime', in *Wechselwirkungen. Jahrbuch 1991. Aus Lehre und Forschung der Universität Stuttgart*, Stuttgart: 1991, pp. 83-95, esp. p. 90f.
8. Max Domarus, Hitler, *Reden and Proklamationen 1932-1945 Kommentiert von einem deutschen Zeitgenossen*. Vol. 2, Part 1, 1939-1940, Wiesbaden: 1973, p. 1058.

## REFERENCES

Bauer, Yehuda, *The Holocaust in Historical Perspective*, Seattle: 1978.

———, *Jews for Sale? Nazi-Jewish Negotiations, 1933-1945*, Yale: 1994.

Benz Wolfgang (ed.), *Die Juden in Deutschland 1933-1945. Leben unter nationalsozialistischer Herrschaft*, München: 1988.

———, *Das Exil der kleinen Leute. Alltagserfahrung deutscher Juden in der Emigratiom*, München: 1988.

Dawidowicz, Lucy S., *The War against the Jews, 1933-1945*, New York: 1975.

Fleming, Gerald, *Hitler and the Final Solution,* London: 1985.
Hilberg, Raul, *The Destruction of the European Jews,* Chicago: 1967.
Jäckel, Eberhard and Jürgen Rohwer (eds.), *Der Mord an den Juden im Zweiten Weltkrieg,* Stuttagart: 1985.
Kwiet, Konrad (ed.), *From the Emancipation to the Holocaust: Essays on Jewish Literature and History in Central Europe,* Kensingon (NSW): 1987.
Marrus, Michael R., *The Unwanted European Refugees in the Twentieth Century,* New York and Oxford: 1985.
Schleunes, Karl A., *The Twisted Road to Auschwitz: Nazi Policy toward German Jews 1933-1939,* Urbana and Chicago: 1990.
Seger, Tom, *Die Siebte Million,* Hamburg: 1995.
Wasserstein, Bernard, *Britain and the Jews of Europe 1939-1945,* Oxford : 1979.

# POLICIES AND RESPONSES

# British Policy towards German-speaking Emigrants in India 1939 -1945

*Joachim Oesterheld*

## THE VISA ISSUE

When the denunciation of the Anglo-German visa agreement became effective from 21 May 1938, the holders of valid German passports required a British visa for entry in the United Kingdom and into British colonies.[1] A similar rule was effective for holders of valid Austrian passports from 2 May 1938. The main purpose of the visa was 'to regulate the flow into the United Kingdom of persons who, for political, racial or religious reasons, may wish to take refuge there in considerable numbers. . . . Even if they are not personally undesirable, the admission in large [*sic*] numbers of refugees who have no resources and no definite prospects would create serious economic and social problems. The test should be whether or not an applicant is likely to be an asset to the United Kingdom. . . .[2] There were special instructions in the circular issued by the Passport Control Department of the Foreign Office dated 28 April 1938 for cases which should be referred as well as for those cases where a visa was granted without reference.

At the end of 1938 there was an increasing pressure of applications for visas permitting entry into British India, mainly by German and Austrian Jews terrorized after the *Anschluss* of Austria and as a consequence of the *Reichskristallnacht* in Germany. British policy restricted admission to India even to those persons who had a chance to enter the country as they were found not to be politically undesirable and to have friends or relations in India who would guarantee their permanent maintenance. The aim was to prevent the immigrants from becoming destitute and a burden upon the country while it was at the same time, 'ordinarily desirable that visas should be granted to them both on humanitarian grounds and because many of them are persons of high qualifications and ability'.[3] For obtaining a visa it was necessary that an unrestricted guarantee for permanent maintenance be given by a reliable British or non-British resident in India for an unlimited period. Even where a contract for several years of employment with a responsible Indian firm had been promised, this form of guarantee was a necesssary precondition.

As such a procedure limited the chances of immigration into India of many German and Austrian applicants, and also of those who stayed with a limited permission in other European countries, the Council for German Jewry in London approached the India Office in late 1938. The India Office authorities were asked to amend the terms of guarantee and to accept also a guarantee given by a responsible Jewish body in India. It was proposed to grant visas to near relatives of residents of German Jewish origin in India, if the former were willing to support their relations in case the need arose. Visas should be granted to prospective immigrants, who possessed a contract for at least two years of employment with a firm in India, even to those persons without any means of supporting themselves but with a guarantee for maintenance by a refugee relief organization in India.

After consultations with the Government of India an arrangement was agreed upon by the India Office and the Council for German Jewry according to which the latter would send names of refugees to the Jewish Relief Association in Bombay with the request to offer the required guarantees for them. In case of a positive reply, the council was to inform the India Office about the names of applicants to whom visas for India may be granted. For practical reasons, however, the Jewish Relief Association dealt directly with the Government of India, which notified the Secretary of State about the names of applicants, so that the necessary instructions could be issued to the passport authorities concerned.[4]

From January 1938 up to the first week of February 1939, the Government of India sanctioned the grant of visas to 269 Jewish refugees, among them 128 women and 16 children. It was not known how many of them had arrived in India. The debates in the Legislative Assembly and Indian press reports at the beginning of 1939, expressed apprehensions about a presumed 'unrestricted immigration' of refugees having an adverse effect on the professional life of Indians. The Government of India denied any large-scale immigration of

German professionals and expected the total number of refugees to compete for employment in India to be not more than 150 persons.[5]

Mounting pressure from various quarters complaining about the competition of these refugees with Indians in various professions and in business caused the Government of India to give further consideration to the question of imposing a limit on the number of refugees admitted into the country. In its letter of 18 May 1939, to the provincial governments and local administrations, the Government of India gave notice 'that as from the middle of May 1939 the number of wage earners (as distinct from dependents) to whom visas will be authorised should be limited to two hundred'.[6]

Immediately after the outbreak of the Second World War in 1939, the Government of India found it necessary to modify its policy with regard to the admission of refugees. As a general rule, visas were issued only to those refugees who, in addition to fulfilling the conditions previously laid down, had been granted admission to the United Kingdom.[7] Further restrictions were inposed in summer 1940, when the Government of India visualized 'danger to security arising from the possible introduction into India of enemy agents in the guise of refugees from Germany'. It was decided 'not to authorise the grant of visas in future to Jewish refugees of enemy nationality whether they have been admitted to the United Kingdom or not'. The grant of visas to the dependents of refugees already in India which so far had been permitted in certain cases as an exception to the general rule was also stopped.[8]

## CONTROL OF FOREIGNERS

Taking into consideration developments in Europe during the year 1938, the Government of India started preparations for dealing with foreigners in the event of a war in early 1939 itself. On 29 March army headquarters issued a memorandum with 'instructions for the disposal of enemy aliens arrested by the civil power on the outbreak of war'. It was decided that in the event of a war the Defence Department of the Government of India would undertake responsibility for the accommodation and custody of enemy aliens whereas the arrests would be made by civil authorities. Before legislation were introduced, military authorities would approach local civil authorities to obtain from them the estimated numbers of aliens, and the Central Government asked the provincial governments to cooperate on this point.

In the event of a war, the policy of the Government of India towards enemy aliens would be to intern all male persons of the age of 16 and above, while females and males below that age would not be interned unless there were definite reasons for such an action. After local detention for a period not exceeding 22 days, they would be transferred to central internment camps. Figures of 1000 European and 2500 Asiatic civilians were anticipated for internment where they would be dealt with in different categories.[9]

There were a number of legal provisions before the outbreak of war. While in the United Kingdom the internment of enemy subjects was effected in exercise of the Royal Prerogative, in India all restrictions on foreigners rested on statutory provisions. After the Registration of Foreigners Act was passed in summer of 1939, the Government of India requested the provincial governments, in July 1939, to provide relevant statistics relating to the total number of registered foreigners on the basis of nationalities; the Government of India wanted complete lists of German, Italian and Japanese subjects with their names, sex, occupation and the districts in which they were registered and, finally, a list of all consular staff.[10] In mid-July 1939 there were 2153 registered persons resident in Bombay (excluding consular staff and persons below l6), among them 1051 Europeans (550 Germans only), 886 Asiatics, 211 Americans and 5 Africans.[11] The total number in Bengal on 31 July 1939 was 1811 persons, among them 1369 registered in Calcutta, and 442 in the districts. The breakdown in Calcutta was as follows: 267 Japanese, 243 Iraqians, 195 Germans and 138 Americans.[12]

In response to requests made by provincial governments, a memorandum on the control of foreigners at the outbreak of war was sent by the Government of India on 10 August 1939 to the provincial governments with an indication of the measures which would be necessary immediately on the outbreak of war together with suggestions for preparatory action. This memorandum included 'provisional instructions for the control of foreigners in war' with an attached list of 32 local internment camps and the designation of military authorities responsible for the establishment of the camps.[13] Viceroy and Governor-General Linlithgow promulgated the Foreigners Ordinance on 26 August 1939[14] under which on the same day, the Foreigners Order was published prohibiting the entry and departure of any foreigner into or out of the country. It also prohibited the presence of foreigners in certain places and their employment or presence in premises used by any public utility and other specified undertakings. The Foreigners Order was amended on 2 September 1939, empowering the civil authorities to arrest any foreigner without a warrant and to detain him.

The Enemy Foreigners Order, issued on 3 September, placed general restrictions on enemy aliens. It prohibited the departure of male enemy foreigners without permission from the Central Government and forbade an enemy foreigner to change his address without prior permission. Other provisions included a restirction on travelling more than 5 miles without permit, and reporting his or her presence every 24 hours. Certain articles were prohibited, such as cameras, telephones, field glasses, motor-cars and maps. All male enemy foreigners of 16 years or more were to be arrested and interned. Military instructions for the internment of enemy aliens in the event of war preceded these Ordinances and Orders at the end of August 1939.[15]

## INTERNMENT OF ENEMY ALIENS

In a circular despatched before the outbreak of war, the British Government reacted to inquiries by colonial governments for advice with regard to the treatment of enemy aliens in time of war. In view of the diverse conditions existing in the various countries, it was thought best 'not to attempt to suggest any policy applicable to all Dependencies'. The memorandum enclosed pointed out that it was 'not proposed to carry out in this country any general internment of enemy aliens at the outbreak of hostilities'.[16] Thus, it was left to the Government of India to decide its own procedure in the light of that policy and with due regard to local conditions.

On 3 September 1939, the Government of India interned all male enemy subjects, i.e. German and Austrian Jewish refugees and all German and Austrian subjects including missionaries. Holders of Czechoslovakian passports, with a few exceptions, were not interned, and the consular staff of enemy countries was also excluded. Women and children under 16 years were exempted too. The internees were removed to local camps and later on transferred to the central internment camp at Ahmednagar. A press release of 26 September 1939 mentions that out of the 1500 Germans in India, some 850 had been arrested for internment.[17]

The exact total figure of all the interned enemy subjects at

Ahmednagar, including 8 persons received from Burma, was 888. In addition, there were 21 persons interned but released from local internment camps before the transfer to Ahmednagar started. In cases of male internees not in a position to make provision for their wives and children and these dependents being unable to support themselves, the Government of India, on application, granted a monthly allowance of Rs. 70, except in Bombay and Calcutta where the maximum was Rs. 80 a month. The monthly allowance for a child was Rs. 30.[18]

For various reasons the policy of wholesale internment pursued by the Government of India did not find undivided support by the British Government including the India Office. Immediately after the outbreak of war the British Govemment had approached the US Government with the request to use that country's Embassy's good offices in Berlin to facilitate the departure of British subjects from Germany. The US Government on its own initiated negotiations regarding the general treatment of enemy subjects with a view to obviating the unnecessary hardships suffered by individuals in the last War. It was in this context that the policy of the Government of India vis-à-vis German subjects resident in India became relevant.

The German Foreign Office through a memorandum, replied on 11 September to a note by the US Embassy:

> The German Government in its special measures against British subjects has been governed solely by the attitude of the British Government towards German citizens. According to reliable information, the authorities of the British colonies have taken steps to intern German citizens. The German Government is however ready in principle to allow British subjects to leave Germany on the basis of reciprocity. It should be hereby understood that free departure will be rendered possible also to German citizens who are residing in British India, the British colonies and protectorates as well as in the mandated territories.... As soon as the German Government receives assurances in this respect, it will permit British subjects to depart from Germany.[19]

The number of British subjects in Germany in September 1939 was 3490, out of which 2725 belonged to the United Kingdom and 107 to India.[20]

On 16 September 1939, the Foreign Office asked the India Office to inform them about the situation of German citizens in India and suggested 'that any statement of the position should include an assurance that there is no intention to intern women and children and that German citizens are not at present being "rounded up" into places of concentration'.[21] Besides the Home and Foreign Offices, the India Office also felt 'that the general internment policy which India adopted, however convenient from the point of view of security in Indian conditions, is going to prove somewhat embarrassing to His Majesty's Government'.[22]

The Government of India interned a number of refugees who were en route to Australia and confiscated their ship on 3 September in Bombay. As international opinion was likely to be interested in the treatment of refugees of German nationality, such a measure, it was feared, would definitely affect neutral opinion in the United States of America and elsewhere. The treatment of German missionaries in particular could have a similar impact. By mid-October, after consultation with the Foreign and Home Offices, the India Office felt that the Government of India should reconsider the policy of general internment in relation to German nationals.

This policy change was also influenced by suggestions submitted to the India Office by the High Commissioner for Refugees of the League of Nations at the beginning of October. He referred to a letter which he had received through the Council of German Jewry, in which the Jewish Relief Association in Bombay, on 16 September, had asked the Government of India to explain the reasons why the refugees in India were treated differently from those in England. 'The Association does not claim to know the history of every individual', the letter states for the very reason that,

> many of the refugees arrived here on visas not sponsored by them, but the majority are known to the Committee and they have no hesitation in assuring the Government of India that these gentlemen are loyal and anxious to become British subjects as soon as possible, and several of the young men would, they believe, be glad of the opportunity to offer themselves for active service. A further point ... is the humiliation caused to the Jewish refugees by being interned together with German Nazis, who are responsible for their persecution, the break-up of their homes and careers and the loss of all their property.

The High Commissioner in his letter to the India Office stressed the point that the procedure adopted in Great Britain 'is to distinguish genuine refugees from others, and for this purpose Tribunals have been set up. I would suggest for the consideration of the Government of India that a similar procedure be followed there'.[23]

A similar line of approach prevailed in the India Office by end of

September 1939, as revealed by the following communication to the Foreign Office:

It would appear possible that there are in the first place individuals or possibly classes amongst those interned who could, without danger, be permitted to remain at liberty in India if they desire to do so; and if such cases are found to exist it seems desirable that the persons concerned should not be put to the inconvenience of a longer period of detention than is strictly necessary.[24]

The Foreign Office, eager to fall in line with the proposals of the US Government, stressed in its reply to the India Office,

that the Government of the United States has condemned the wholesale internment of enemy civilians and that His Majesty's Government propose to give an assurance that every case will be considered on its individual merits. It would weaken the position of His Majesty's Government if it were necessary to admit that all male Germans over sixteen had been interned in India without reference to the merits of individual cases, unless it could at the same time be represented that this measure was in the nature of a precaution and subject to early revision.[25]

With the backing of the Foreign Office, the India Office, in a lengthy letter, urged the Government of India in mid-October to

consider modification of your internment policy somewhat on lines adopted in United Kingdom and Colonies, i.e. that you should discriminate between first, enemy aliens who might without danger be permitted to remain at liberty in India especially for example missionaries, secondly those who might with due precautions be repatriated if they so desire, and thirdly residue [*sic*] who must be kept in internment for reasons of state.

The India Office also submitted a suggested statement which it asked the Government of India to authorize as 'this will remove a source of embarrassment to His Majesty's Government in their negotiations on behalf of British subjects now in Germany'.[26]

It took the Government of India a fortnight to state its position regarding the treatment of aliens. While it agreed to the proposals for a statement by the Government of the United Kingdom, with minor modifications, it defended its radical policy of internment:

While we are anxious to fall into line with policy of His Majesty's Government, we are constrained to emphasise essential differences between conditions in India and United Kingdom. We are separated only by land frontiers from States where enemy powers are known to have set up centres for creating trouble in India and considerable section of our population is, unlike England, actually or potentially disloyal.[27]

The proposals which the Government of India finally accepted in order to secure uniformity in different parts of the British empire required a review of the cases not only of Jewish refugees but also of all enemy internees with a view to releasing those who were not likely to be a danger to security and to renounce any intention of compulsory repatriation of women and other enemy subjects at liberty. When the British Government in November 1939 accepted the proposals of the State Department of the United States of America, there was a particular reference to India:

As regards India it will be appreciated that special circumstances affecting internal and external security have necessitated greater caution in the application of this policy than in the United Kingdom. The Government of India have, however, also accepted the general principles set out . . . in determining their policy towards German nationals in India. In pursuance of these principles a special committee which was set up in September is considering the case of every person temporarily detained on its individual merits, and had already by the end of October ordered or recommended the release of 160; every alien whose internment is recommended by the committee will be granted a right of appeal to the competent authority which will be decided on its merits.[28]

The special committee which was appointed to interrogate internees at the central internment camp at Ahmednagar became known as Darling Committee for Interrogation of Alien Internees. This committee, under Sir Malcolm Darling with W.O. Wood, and from December 1939 with J. Abernethy as additional member, completed its work in April 1940. Up to mid-November 1939 it ordered the release of 309 refugees and 19 others, including 4 missionaries. It was then decided to investigate the cases of all other internees to find out in each case whether or not the individual could be released from internment.[29] As a result 561 male German subjects were released by the committee; Among these, 330 persons were treated as Jewish refugees and 123 as missionaries or priests.[30]

Some refugees faced difficulties after their release from Ahmednagar as they could not find re-employment. In December 1939 the Government of India thought it appropriate to clarify that

while the fact that an individual refugee has been released cannot be taken as a complete guarantee of trustworthiness, it may be taken as an indication that Government consider that he need not be regarded as a dangerous person. Employers and others who may have doubts about the desirability of re-employing released refugees or re-admitting them to various forms of social life are, therefore, advised not to allow the mere fact that such persons were arrested and temporarily interned to create a prejudice against them. If, however, an employer who is engaged in a business involving Government contracts, particularly contracts relating to defence and security undertakings, has doubts about re-employing any particular released refugee, he should seek the advice of the Provincial or of the Central Government.[31]

For many released internees an additional reason for not finding employment was the closing down of so-called, 'enemy firms', where they had been employed before the outbreak of war. Therefore, already in late December 1939, the Government of India examined 'the possibility of establishing some sort of settlement in which released internees and their families may, if they are destitute, be accommodated until such time, if ever, as they return to Germany, or can support themselves here'.[32]

The old military hill station at Purandhar (Maharashtra) was earmarked for such a family camp. Its conversion for this purpose, however, was suspended, because as long as the Darling Committee had not concluded its work, it was not possible to estimate the number of persons the camp was to house. When, later on, it turned out that the number of persons to be released from military custody was too small, the proposal to establish a family camp was abandoned.

The number of those who wanted to, and could be allowed to, return to Germany was negligible. By the end of December 1939, the India Office was 'entirely in the dark on the whole question of repatriation' and pressed the Government of India to give 'even the most rudimentary estimate of the probable numbers' and to let them know 'from week to week what numbers of women and children are actually leaving India and particulars of ships and routes and measures taken to ensure their reaching their ultimate destination'.[33]

After the amendment of the Enemy Foreigners Order in February 1940, all German subjects had to obtain permission to depart which, till then, was required for males only. A German subject was allowed to leave British India only through the port of Bombay and permits would restrict the direct journey by sea from Bombay to Italy via the Red Sea. Among the Germans who left India immediately after the outbreak of war in October and November were the staff members of the Consulates in Calcutta and Bombay including the Consul-Generals Count Dönhoff and Dr. Pausch totalling 11 men and 6 women. The overall figure of 173 Germans allowed to depart from British India until summer 1940 comprised 31 men, 96 women and 46 children.[34]

RE-INTERNMENT

After the Darling Committee completed its work in spring 1940, out of some 1800 German and Austrian subjects resident in India at the outbreak of the war, some 600 males were at liberty, of whom about 370 were refugees and 230 were of various categories including missionaries. In addition, about 770 female German and Austrian subjects stayed in India, of whom 450 were independent (mainly nuns), 280 were dependent upon refugees and other released internees and the remaining 40 were the wives of persons still interned.[35] The situation drastically changed with the German invasion of Denmark, Norway, Holland and Belgium and the collapse of France.

As in the United Kingdom the authorities in British India likewise took great care in rounding up enemy subjects at liberty. The Government of India referred also to misgivings expressed by certain provincial governments about the presence of released internees and, in this context, criticized the work of the Darling Committee, for which the possibility of error due to insufficient information should be recognized. The government claimed 'that humanitarian considerations which, in pursuance of certain international agreements, underlay the appointment of the committee may in some cases have influenced their decisions to a greater extent than was justified'.[36] The re-examination of the cases of released internees started at once providing for the internment of any non-missionary or non-refugee male about whom the local authorities were not satisfied. The arrest and internment of any individual missionary or refugee who had given cause for suspicion were not excluded.

The attitudes or perceptions of governors with respect to this new line of action reveal an atmosphere charged with fear, hatred and distress. The Governor of Madras Province reported that 'there is a widespread feeling that far too much latitude has [been] and is being given. The Darling Committee seems to have taken an extraordinary line and let out Nazi sympathisers wholesale. We have seen what "fifth column", activities can do, in Norway and Holland, and although the position is different here, they can [do] and are doing harm by their defeatist activities.'[37]

His counterpart in Bombay Province apprehended 'fear of Hitlerism . . . overshadowing internal politics'. In the North-West Province's report the people appeared 'genuinely distressed and frightened by news of German success' and educated classes expected the government to take 'special measures to protect India from enemy attack'.[38]

In Assam, however, where the bulk of enemy subjects consisted of Italian missionaries running schools, orphanages and other institutions, the Governor's report cautioned that 'the immediate internment elsewhere of the whole lot would cause great hardship and inconvenience' and that there was 'considerable criticism of the policy'.[39]

The Government of India regarded close internment in many cases and particularly in the case of women as not necessary as it felt little or no reason to suspect either nuns or the majority of the dependents of refugees. Nevertheless, the presence of wives of internees was regarded as embarrassing, and 'this class of women in particular should no longer be allowed to reside freely in the ports or in any other place of political or strategic importance or where troops are stationed. . . . This suggests the ultimate formation of what may be termed parole settlements which, in the first place at least, could most conveniently be established on a provincial basis.'[40]

Provincial governments opened parole centres at the following places: Satara (Bombay Province), Naini Tal (United Provinces), Hazaribagh (Bihar), Katapahar (Bengal), Shillong (Assam), and Yarkand and Kodaikanal (Madras Province). There were no suitable places in the Punjab since hill stations were either cantonments or important places

> where the presence of enemy women could not be permitted. We decided therefore, largely in order to meet the Punjab's requirements to open a parole centre at Purandhar. . . . It was also our intention so far as possible to segregate Jewish refugees at Purandhar. . . . German Aryan and Italian women whom we do not consider it desirable to allow to reside in important strategical centres like Bombay have now been removed to Satara.[41]

As far as the treatment of refugees was concerned, the Government of India consulted the provincial governments, and as their opinion was that general security demanded that all refugees be segregated, it instructed them 'that individuals suspected of enemy sympathy should be interned and that the remaining refugees who were suspect only on general grounds . . . should be removed to parole settlements'.[42]

On 31 August 1940, 2186 Germans and Austrians were in British India either in internment, parole centres or at liberty. According to categories used by the Home Department of the Government of India, 501 male persons were interned (including 33 missionaries and 38 refugees), and 409 persons were confined to parole settlements (including 60 male and 16 female missionaries and 82 male and

89 female refugees). The number of persons at liberty was 1276 (which included 303 male and 303 female missionaries and 257 male and 229 female refugees). These figures indicate that in summer 1940 there were at least 695 (all Jewish?) refugees among the 2186 people from Germany and Austria. We do not know exactly but have to assume that children have been included in the figures.[43] When the policy of radical internment met with a growing opposition in the United Kingdom in July 1940 and the British Government issued a White Book with 18 categories of persons eligible for release from internment by the end of that month, the Government of India came again under pressure to follow suit. The Calcutta branch of the Jewish Relief Association sent a telegram on 16 July to the German Jewish Aid Committee in London and suggested 'immediate Representation be made either to Secretary of State for India or by Parliamentary questions for Indian Government to be directed to follow English Policy'.[44] On the basis of this telegram the High Commissioner for Refugees approached the India Office and stressed the necessity not to confuse refugees with non-refugee enemy aliens, because refugees 'are victims of Nazi oppression and therefore opposed to the Nazi regime'.[45]

The India Office informed the Government of India about the policy change of the British Government towards enemy aliens on 31 July. The former expected the latter to realize 'the importance of keeping your policy as closely as possible in line with policy here' and suggested 'setting up again a small standing committee to consider and advise you on treatment of individual cases'.[46] By the end of September, the Government of India reviewed its policy regarding refugees of enemy nationality and adopted nine categories of persons eligible for exemption out of which eight categories were applicable only to refugees of enemy origin and the last one to all enemy aliens, whether refugees or not.[47]

An Aliens Advisory Committee was set up with G.B. Constantine as chairman and Sir David Devadoss, Sir Mohammad Yamin Khan, Lieutenant Colonel L.G.V. Hamber and A.G. Phillips as members. It reviewed the cases of all refugees and Jews of enemy nationality who might be eligible for release from restriction or for continuance at liberty under any of the nine categories. In December 1940 four categories were added based upon communications received from the India Office. The committee assembled on 14 October 1940 and the members handed over charge on 18 February 1941.

The committee found the interpretation of the categories difficult as such interpretation resulted in anomalies and their strict application would have increased the detained population. The committee recommended the abandonment of the category system in respect of Jewish refugees, and their restraint or liberty should be governed solely by considerations of security. It felt that 'in the absence of reasons to the contrary it should be presumed that a refugee is entitled to his liberty'.[48]

Before the Government of India took a decision the Jewish Relief Association submitted its position on the refugee question. The main line of argument was to point to 'a fundamental difference between Jewish refugees in the United Kingdom and refugees out here'[India]. The difference was not only with respect to numbers, but also with respect to the conditions under which refugees found shelter and lived.

As labour permits were granted only in exceptional cases in England, e.g. where the majority of refugees was not in a position to start new lives and careers, the association concluded, that on the whole, refugees in England could not be regarded as settled in the country. In India, however, visas were granted to refugees not only to allow the individual to enter the country, but also provided for the possibility to seek employment or set up business. Those who had managed to come 'regard India as a new home, which would enable them to start life afresh and to build up a future for themselves and for their families'.[49]

In the light of the recommendations of the Aliens Advisory Committee and the attitude of the Jewish Relief Association, the Executive Council accepted new principles stating 'that the category system should be abandoned, that considerations of security should be substituted as the criterion and that in so doing the presumption should be in favour of the refugee'.[50] The adoption of these principles involved an examination of each case on its merits, subject to the understanding that no person in respect of whom the slightest doubt existed should be allowed his liberty until the security services were convinced that there was no longer any ground for suspicion.

Towards the end of December 1941, the Government of India was asked to accept for internment some 2600 Japanese internees from Singapore as well as from Burma and Ceylon (now called Sri Lanka) and almost, at the same time, received a request from the Netherlands authorities to accept 2400 more Germans from the Dutch-ruled East Indies. It was then decided that the Home Department should become responsible for the establishment, organization and administration of camps for these 5000 additional internees. At the same time, the responsibility for the central internment camp at Dehra Dun was also transferred to the Home Department.

The Japanese internees were originally accommodated in a temporary camp at the Purana Qila (Old Fort) in New Delhi and the Germans from the East Indies were held by the military authorities in a prisoners of war camp at Ramgarh. As a result of the loss of one shipment and the re-classification as prisoners of war and the despatch to Canada of 595 of those Germans, their number was reduced to 1325. However, before the extension of the camp at Dehra Dun was complete in order to accommodate all European internees, the military situation required that the German internees be removed from Ramgarh. They were eventually accommodated at Deoli (Rajasthan) from July 1942 until April 1943, then transferred to Dehra Dun, and their place at Deoli was taken by the Japanese internees.[51]

By August 1943, there were 1724 German-speaking and 558 Italian subjects among the 2551 internees in Dehra Dun.[52] The German internees had markings in the security nominal rolls ranging from X to XXXX. 'Anti-nazi or Anti-fascist' was indicated by X. Double X was a marking for 'Generally speaking, in varying degrees, Nazi and Fascist sympathisers until the defeat of Germany and Italy but who always have been very moderate in their opinions and who have taken no definite interest in political activities during internment'. The third category (XXX) was a designated 'definite Nazis and Fascists until defeat of Germany and Italy but who now have apparently become more moderate and sensible in their opinions. This category includes many opportunists.' The last category (XXXX )was for 'strong and still convinced Nazis or Fascists who are likely to exert a bad influence if given the opportunity'.[53]

After the fall of Singapore, when the Japanese Army approached India's frontiers, the Government of India, after consulting general headquarters' closed the parole centres at Katapahar, Shillong, Yarkand, Kodaikanal and Hazaribagh and transferred their population to the parole centres at Purandhar and Satara, while unmarried male persons went to internment camps. Missionaries and nuns were under special orders, while 111 male and 85 female Jewish refugees were allowed to stay on in the threatened areas of the Eastern and Southern Commands of the Army.[54] The parole centre at Nainital too was closed down and its inmates transferred to Purandhar and Satara, which were expanded in 1942 to absorb parolees from the other centres being closed down. For that purpose they were transformed into combined family internment camps and parole centres. Purandhar had a preponderance of Jewish and half-Jewish refugees whose applications for release had been rejected or who had failed to secure employment and, for that reason, were still detained.[55] The non-Jewish German-speaking population in India in spring 1942 totalled1002 persons, comprising 547 males over 18 years old (422 interned, 79 at liberty and 46 in parole centres) and 455 females (341 at liberty, 114 in parole centres).[56]

## POST-WAR DEVELOPMENTS

When the war was over, the Government of India's policy towards foreigners still in detention differentiated between those sent from abroad for detention in India and those who had been resident in India prior to detention. As far as the first category was concerned, it was proposed to repatriate them to their own countries or to the countries from which they were received.Those in the second category, irrespective of their political attitude, were not to be released in India. They were to be repatriated compulsorily but applications for individual relaxation were admitted. A similar policy was applied to enemy foreigners restricted to parole centres. However, for enemy foreigners at liberty, all restrictions were removed and they were treated as ordinary foreigners subject only to the Registration of Foreigners Act, 1939.[57]

In February 1946 the British Government dealt, in particular, with those Germans who, for political reasons or because of racist persecution, had left Germany after the Nazi assumption of power and had been accepted in India and other colonies. It was recognized that many of them had rendered valuable services to the Allied cause during the war. The British Government expressed the view 'that such persons should generally be permitted to remain in the Colonial territory to which they were originally admitted'.[58] In cases where such refugees were interned they should also generally be permitted to stay on.

The Foreigners Act expired on 30 September 1946. It had provided legal cover for the internment of civilian persons.This wartime provision would have been out of place in a new permanent legislation. The Government of India, therefore, was interested in a repatriation before September 1946.[59] In summer of 1946 the internment camp and parole centre at Purandhar was closed down along with the internment camp at Satara. The inmates of the latter were transferred to the parole centre there and declared parolees, while Satara too finally closed down on 30 April 1947.[60]

In spring 1947 the total number of German internees and parolees left in India was less than 100. While the Indian chapter for these Germans came to an end with their compulsory repatriation, many of the refugees from Germany and Austria did not return to the places from where they had been forced to leave after 1933. The archival material is silent about their daily life patterns in India apart from the periods of internment and reinternment. Such patterns have yet to be reconstructed as their fate should not be forgotten.

## NOTES AND REFERENCES

1. This article is the first attempt to reconstruct the political and legal framework under which the Jewish refugees from Central Europe found asylum in India. The author is grateful for assistance by the National Archives of India, New Delhi; the West Bengal State Archives, Calcutta; the Tamil Nadu Archives, Chennai; the Maharashtra State Archives, Mumbai; and the India Office Library and Records, London. The following abbreviations are used: GoM—Government of Madras, IOR—India Office Records; MSA—Maharashtra State Archives; NAI—National Archives of India; GoI—Government of India; SAWB—State Archives of West Bengal; TA—Tamil Nadu Archives.
2. Circular Passport Control Department, Foreign Office, 27 April 1938, p. 3. NAI, Home Department, Political Section file no. 46/17/38—Political.
3. Letter, GoI, Home Department no. 17/407/38—Political, 21 January 1939. TA, Political and Services Department file no. 2456/34.
4. Letter, Council for German Jewry to India Office, 12 December 1938 and letter, India Office to Council for German Jewry, 3 January 1939. NAI, Home Department, Political Section file no. 17/415/38—Political. The history of the Jewish Relief Association in Bombay has not yet been written and its records have not been traced so far. The association made a selfless contribution to providing shelter for hundreds of German and Austrian refugees in India and in assisting them on their way to Shanghai.
5. Letter, home member of Council of the Governor-General to Chief Secretary to Government of Bombay, 23 February 1939. MSA, Political and Services Department file no. 2636/34.

6. Letter, GoI, Home Department no. 17/140/39—Political, 18 May 1939. TA, GoM 2933, Home Department, 27 May 1939.
7. Letter, GoI, Home Department no. 17/140/39—Political, 15 September 1939. MSA, Political and Services Department file no. 2456/34.
8. Letter, GoI, Home Department no. 17/358/40—Political, 15 July 1940. TA, GoM 3158, Home Department, 29 July 1940.
9. Army Headquarters, India. no. B/51702/A.G.-XI. NAI, Home Department, Political Section, file no. 21/4/39.
10. Letter GoI, Home Department no. 22/50/39—Political, 21 July 1939. SAWB, Home (Political) Department Conf. file no. 390/39.
11. *The Times of India*, Bombay, 18 and 19 July 1939.
12. Number of foreigners registered in Calcutta up to 14 August 39. SAWB, Home (Political) Department. Conf. file no. 390/39.
13. Letter, GoI, Home Department no. 21/4/49—Political, 10 August 1939. NAI, Home Department, Political Section file no. 21/4/39. There was a revised list of local internment camps, end of August (Letter, GoI, Home Department no. 21/4/39—Political(W), 26 August 1939. SAWB, Home (Political) Department Conf. file no. 408/39.
14. For this Ordinance and the following Orders mentioned, cf. IOR, L/P+J/8/41, Coll. 101/10B.
15. Military Instructions for the Internment of Enemy Aliens in the Event of War, 1939 (Provisional) General Staff, India, Simla, 25 August1939. IOR, L/P+J/8/30A, Coll. 101/10A.
16. Secret Circular Foreign Office. London, 2 September 1939. IOR, L/P+J/8/65, Coll. 101/12A.
17. Press release, Principal Information Officer, GoI, no. 79/7/39-Pub. 26 September 1939. IOR, ibid. As the Government of India did not differentiate between German and Austrian citizens the figure includes persons from both the countries. As an exemption German and Austrian Jews were not arrested in Bengal on 3 September. There were instructions by the governor according to which refugees against whom there was no suspicion should not be arrested (telegram, Viceroy to India Office. New Delhi, 12 October 1939. IOR, ibid.).
18. Legislative Assembly Debates, New Delhi, 8 February 1940. IOR, L/P+J/8/66, Coll 101/12B.
19. Letter, US Embassy in London, 12 September 1939, to Foreign Office. IOR, L/P+J/8/65, Coll. 101/12A.
20. Note, German Foreign Office to US Embassy in Berlin, 24 April 1940. IOR, L/P+J/8/66, Coll 101/12B. According to a decree from 7 September 1939, all nationals of Great Britain, Northern Ireland, British colonies, protectorates, mandates and India who were in Germany had to register in person with the local police within 24 hours and were not allowed to leave the localities without police permission (Information from US Embassy in London to Foreign Office from

9 September 1939. IOR, L/P+J/8/65, Coll. 101/12A). In April 1940 the number of Indians left in Germany was 36 with four children and none was interned (letter, Foreign Office to India Office, London 16 April 1940. IOR, L/P+J/8/66, Coll. 101/12B).

21. Letter, Foreign Office to India Office, London, 16 September 1939. IOR, L/P+J/8/65. Coll. 101/12A.
22. India Office, Public and Judicial Department (Minute Paper). IOR, ibid.
23. Letter, High Commissioner for Refugees to the Under-Secretary of State for India, London, 3 October 1939. IOR, ibid.
24. Draft letter, India Office to Foreign Office, London, 26 September 1939. IOR, ibid.
25. Letter, Foreign Office to India Office, London, 9 October 1939. IOR, ibid.
26. Letter, India Office to GoI, London, 13 October 1939. IOR, ibid.
27. Telegram, GoI to the India Office, New Delhi, 31 October1939. IOR, ibid.
28. Aide memoire Government of United Kingdom, London, 24 November, 1939. IOR, ibid.
29. Press note, GoI, New Delhi, 20 November 1939. IOR, ibid.
30. Letter, GoI, Home Department no. 62/22/40—Political(W), 19 May 1940. IOR, L/P+J/8/66, Coll. 101 /12B.
31. Press note, GoI, New Delhi, 20 December 1939. IOR, ibid.
32. Letter, GoI, Home Department no. 21/71/39—Political(W), 28 December 1939.
33. Letter, India Office, P+J 6829/39 to GoI, London, 23 December 1939. IOR, ibid.
34. Draft letter, India Office to Foreign Office, London, 10 June 1940. IOR, ibid.
35. Letter, GoI, Home Department no. 62/22/40—Political (W), Simla 19 May 1940. IOR, ibid.
36. Ibid.
37. Extract from Madras Governor's Report dated 20 May 1940. IOR, ibid.
38. Telegram, Governor-General to Secretary of State for India, Simla, 22 May 1940. IOR, ibid.
39. Extract from Assam: Governor's situation report dated 17 July 1940, no. 68. IOR, ibid.
40. Letter, GoI, Home Department no. 62/22/40. IOR, ibid.
41. Letter, GoI, Home Department to India Office, Simla, 20 September 1940. IOR, ibid.
42. Telegram, GoI to Secretary of State for India, Simla, 11 August 1940. IOR, ibid.

43. Letter, GoI, Home Department to India Office, Simla, 20 September 1940. IOR, ibid.
44. Cable, Jewish Refugees Relief Association, Calcutta, 16 July 1940. IOR, ibid.
45. Letter, High Commissioner for Refugees to the Secretary of State for India, London, 5/7 August 1940. IOR, ibid.
46. Telegram, Secretary of State for India to GoI, London, 31 July 1940. IOR, ibid.
47. Telegram, GoI, Home Department to Secretary of State for India, Simla, 30 September 1940. IOR, ibid.
48. Analysis of recommendations of the Aliens Advisory Committee. IOR, ibid.
49. Letter, Jewish Relief Association to the GoI, Bombay, 27 March 1941. IOR, ibid.
50. Meeting of the Executive Council held on Wednesday, 25 June 1941 at 10-30 a.m. IOR, ibid.
51. GoI, Home Department: *Civil Internment Manual*, 1943, Simla, 1943, pp. 6f. IOR, L/P+J/8/30B, Coll. 101/10A.
52. Camp Central d'Internment de Dehra Dun. Visit by M. M. J.A. Rikli and A. de Spindler on 9 to the 13 August 1943. IOR, L/P+J/8/34, Coll. 101/10AB.
53. German Internees in the Central Internment Camp, Dehra Dun. Explanation of markings in the Security Nominal Roll. IOR, L/P+J/8/32, Coll. 101/10AA/1.
54. Telegram, GoI, Home Department to Secretary of State for India, New Delhi, 23 August 1942. IOR, L/P+J/8/32, Coll. 101/10AA.
55. Letter GoI, Home Department to Secretary of State for India, New Delhi, 3 May 1943. IOR, L/P + J/8/34, Coll. 101/10AB.
56. Telegram, GoI, Home Department to Secretary of State for India, New Delhi, 10 March 1942. IOR, L/P+J/8/66, Coll. 101/12B. These figures do not yet include German internees from the Netherlands East Indies.
57. GoI, Home Department letter no. 9/16/45—Political(EW) to India Office, New Delhi, 1 October 1949. IOR, L/P+J/8/30B, Coll. 101/10AI.
58. Circular telegram from the Secretary of State for the Colonies to the Officer Administering the GoI, London, 22 February 1946. IOR, L/P+J/8/35, Coll. 101/10AB.
59. Letter, GoI, Home Department to India Office, New Delhi, 28 May 1946. IOR, ibid.
60. Letters, GoI to India Office, New Delhi, 2 September 1946 and 3 June 1947. IOR, L/P+J/8/33, Coll. 101/10AAII.

# Jews and Central European Nationals in Exile in Colonial India between the Two World Wars

*Majid Hayat Siddiqi*

## A SENSE OF CONTEXT STEREOTYPES AND THE CARRY-OVER OF PREJUDICES, 1910-1920

As the reality of colonialism in the contemporary world did not derive from the fact of exploitation alone or only from being a society subjected to British rule, colonial India's imaginary status stood autonomous. Paradoxically, being British ruled, then, meant being a part of the greater imperial-colonial imagination. Naturally, the Germans figured in that scheme of things as did Austria-Hungary. Other European nationalities looked for, and were involved in the very things that the Raj syndrome was about. They could not exist outside of it, nor beside it, but in it. Yet, as they were not British, that made for some differences. It is within these similarities and differences that several ideological and cultural stereotypes were carried through.[1]

This may be best gauged from certain records of the early decades of this century despite their fragmentary limitations. When, in 1911, a German, Otto Honigmann, wished to visit India and sought permission to go 'wintering' in Baltistan or Ladakh, the colonial administration allowed him his yen for sports but explicitly forbade any surveying of the area. It noted that other Germans had also visited the area lately but remained uncertain as to the status of their own reaction: 'The Germans are showing a remarkable interest in this part of the World. We don't think they are after surveys but have their eyes on the Ladakh–Chinese–Turkestan trade.'[2]

A look at just one other record of the same year pertaining to German interest in India, and the pieces of the imperial-colonial imagination begin to fall into place. Three German nationals, namely, Dr Karl Wolfskehl, 'a Munich artist', Melchior Lechter, 'a well-known painter' and Baron von Bernus, 'an art critic and man of letters, were recommended permission to enter India by Lord Morley at the instance of 'His Royal Highness the Grand Duke of Hesse'.[3] Lechter was reported to have, 'besides others, the hobby of taking an emphatic interest in Occultism and Buddhism and [was as reported] would be perfectly happy if he could get a glimps [sic] of and an interview with the Dalai Lama.'

All the motifs—'Mystic India', the 'imperial eye' of painters, travels into the Great Game, 'sport' and identity, the sublimation of commercial ambitions—that made for the British syndrome[4] are, it may be observed, clearly a part of the practices of the European idea in its co-mingling with the experience of British rule. We even have at least two German or Austrian Miss Questeds, as it were, wishing to visit their very own Marabar caves—at Ellora![5] And Forsterian ambivalence barely veils the gaffes of imperial science when, in 1911, M. Taute of Germany wished to travel to India to carry out 'scientific investigation' into 'sleeping sickness',[6] a disease already established in 1902 as location-specific between certain latitudes of the African continent, contracted from an African 'native' the tse-tse fly (not found in India). With an astonishing simultaneity, other documents of the period record the visits of ethnographers and military men, for instance, L. Scherman, Director of the Ethnographical Museum at Munich,[7] His Royal Highness Prince Antoine d'Orleans and Braganza, Lieutenant in the Imperial and Royal Sixth Regiment of Hussars.[8] Of course, in this overwhelming sense of European identity, the British kept a close watch on their German guests, whether they wished to insist on supervisory police presence for Lechter's interview with the Dalai Lama [9] or simply tailed their movements, as of one H. de Hanke, described as 'a German swindler'.[10]

Beneath the resemblances of the imperial-colonial syndrome lurked the monster of nationalism and national rivalries. Anglo-German rivalry in the years after 1900 is now too well-known in European history to bear the weight of any further emphasis. And, surely, that rivalry also played a crucial part in determining the history of colonial events and mentalities following the outbreak of war. But the point to which we would like to draw attention here is this: the war threw up stereotypes that went beyond the boundaries of the shared syndrome of dominance and rivalry. The imperial-colonial cultural syndrome was about shared ideologies usually vis-à-vis 'the other' of the colonies. World power rivalries, on the other hand, were about modern military strength in Europe, especially in post-Bismarckian Germany and the trading outpost of the empire, especially England's.[11] The reaction of the British colonial regime, however created its own stereotypes that determined how attitudes in British Indian society towards the Germans ought to be regulated. It was such attitudes that entered the nitty-gritty of every-day administration in early twentieth-century India.

The example of this xenophobic trend that hits us with a poignant acuity was located in the princely state of Mysore where a newspaper editor, Miss Dawson an English lady, was allegedly sacked from her post by the durbar, through the intervention of the British resident.[12] Her articles in the *Daily Post*, a local Mysore paper, had in their oblique criticisms of the durbar's policy of employing Germans with more than usual fervour, offended the durbar's political view of things as there had been warnings of an increasing 'German Influence in India'.

Consider this statement:

> Looked at squarely . . . the administration of a Ruling Chief [Mysore] finds Germans essential to its conduct of affairs and, from choice or expediency, it cannot carry on its Agricultural Department without a German in it, it cannot use its much-advertised power scheme to light our streets but a German must be in virtual control, it cannot provide schools for a large section of its residents without German aid and to its Christian population its national tongue cannot express the code and dogma Kultur is attempting to vanquish without a German to translate it.

The sacking was criticized by another newspaper, the *Morning Post*: 'What has come over Englishmen that such incidents as this occur? The German people openly boast and sing of their hatred of England . . . have acted in every part of the British Empire as enemy agents and spies and . . . *their whole nation is one vast conspiracy against us*' (emphasis added).

The emerging and, we believe, rampant stereotype was made even more pointed. According to one source: 'We have abundant evidence that the . . . German missionary in particular is often virulently anti-British . . . at the back of most dangerous propaganda.'[13]

It is but a short hop from this record of 1916 to several appeals in 1918 made from the Vatican by P. Cardinal Gasparri on behalf of the Pope and from Cardinal de Hartmann, Archbishop of Cologne, requesting 'an improvement of the painful hardships which several German missionaries interned in India . . . and in Egypt are suffering'.[14]

A whole nation, its religious missionaries—the Catholic orders of

Protestant Germany!—included, was painted in one broad brush stroke of national prejudice. It was this experience of the First World War that determined attitudes towards all Germans, including Jews, when in the years of their persecution they fled, when they could, to different parts of the world. The notoriety of British appeasement of German Fascism aside, they were not received with unqualified enthusiasm in India either. Not only that. When members of other nationalities, such as the Poles, were accommodated, the terms of their inclusion were also negotiated with an eye to their usefulness to British colonial policy. Such machinations of the colonial state lend an altogether different complexion to the view of British India having been a haven for European exiles. It might be more correct perhaps to say that the very question of European identities itself was in refuge, hiding from the certainty of an insistent moral judgement of history.

## IDENTITIES IN REFUGE: GERMANS, JEWS AND POLES (1934-45)

In order that the point we wish to make here is not misunderstood, we first set out the context for refugee relief work as it was carried out. In 1934 a Jewish Relief Association was organized at Bombay and it was backed by material and political support by the Council of German Jewry which operated as the central office in the British empire for the relief of persecuted Jews.[15] By March 1939 an agreement was concluded between India Office and the Council for German Jewry that the ultimate discretion whether or not to allow entry of Jewish refugees into India would rest with the Government of India and a guarantee for an initial support of five years would be necessary from the Jewish Committee in Bombay.[16] A month before that date, in one instance, as many as 850 Jewish refugees without the fullest documentation had not been allowed to land in Bombay and were sent on to Shanghai the same night.[17] The official record reveals the most stringent remarks on the files regarding the necessity of verification.[18] (No 'boat people' could have come in those years.)

In point of fact, even after the agreement, interrogation and internment of German Jewish nationals could go on even when, as in the case of a person called Israel Minner and his wife, a guarantee of support was furnished by the Jewish Relief Association in Bombay in June 1939.[19] While eventually allowed in, Minner, who had been in concentration camps in Dachau and Buchenwald in Germany until February 1939, was arrested and imprisoned on 3 September 1939 and was released only after further interrogation, after nearly two more months. Little wonder, then, that the Jewish Relief Association had, from time to time, to express its greatest apprehension for the refugees who had already arrived and for whom it stood as guarantor, as will be evident from the following excerpts from a circular issued by A.W. Rosenfeld, Secretary, on 23 September 1939:

> My Committee would like to advise all Jewish Refugees of foreign Nationality that in their own interest it is most desirable for them, to conduct themselves in all matters with the utmost circumspection. . . . They owe this duty also to the government of India which is showing them great consideration and which might come in for criticism if the fact that a number of German citizens are left free comes specially to the public notice. . . . German should on no account be spoken, even amongst themselves, and even over the telephone, and not a word should ever be uttered on political subjects. It would be better to avoid all foreign languages and speak only English, as the average inhabitant of this country is unacquainted with Continental languages and may mistake any language for German [. . .] not only should any sort of loud conduct be avoided but also acts, however correct in ordinary circumstances, which are capable under today's conditions of being misconstrued by mischievous persons.[20]

The rounding up of Germans and all politically suspect aliens in the years after the outbreak of war was a fairly general phenomenon. In a list of 77 internees, dated April 1944, release from British camps was recommended for less than half the number, mostly only if the inmates could find 'suitable' employment. Most were either retained on parole or were recommended further restrictions. This list included the identified names of Jewish and part-Jewish German individuals and their families.[21] If there remains any doubt about the constraining terms of the world of relief, it may be dispelled by the following note of the Intelligence Bureau when considering naturalization appeals in 1940. This was at a time when applications from 'German Jewish refugees [were likely] to increase as a number [would] now be completing their 5 years' qualifying period of residence'.[22] 'In the present troublous [*sic*] times it is often not possible to say with absolute certainty that a national of even a friendly country is harmless and is not acting against British interests. *In the case of Jewish refugees the decision is harder still to arrive at.*'[23] No reasons were given for this exclusive consideration.

British policy towards Polish exiles was not very different but as Polish subordination to German dominance had been preceded, before

Munich and the German-Soviet Pact, by Britain's willingness to protect Poland against impending German aggression, it had a different form. For one, there were skilled technicians, engineers and others who had come to India to earn their living through selling their expertise in a compact with the colonial government or as representatives of Polish firms.[24] A great many of them, perhaps in response to the humiliation imposed upon their country by the Nazis, opted for refugee status by entering into a concord with the intelligence department of the colonial government. Their role was to propagate anti-Nazi sentiments through speeches and pamphlet literature. But the performance of some of these refugees generated great anguish in the intelligence bureaucracy. The attributed cause of this, in the bureaucracy's view in March 1942, was Polish refugee reluctance and, in some cases, reneging on the commitment to be unequivocal in their propaganda efforts, displaying thereby, 'a defeatist mentality'.[25] Three instances of such supposed reneging, as reported, are being cited. They reveal as much, if not more, about the wholly utilitarian manner of the colonial state's policy towards refugees as they do about the mental states of the refugees and their general disposition.[26]

1. Francis Sarnowiec who arrived in India under the Polish engineers' scheme and who is the editor of the *Polish News*, an anti-Axis propaganda organ published in Bombay, recently called together a meeting of the Polish engineers and suggested to them that as they had been brought to India by the British Government they should approach the latter for removal to a safer place as Bombay was in imminent danger. He next approached Professor Jan Mis (employed in this office) and Dr Ludwik Sternbach, who helped him in editing the *Polish News*, and suggested that the three of them should make arrangements to leave India as there was a likelihood of this country falling into the hands of Germany, in which case they would suffer the most, being responsible for the anti-Axis propaganda. As he met with no response he compromised by suggesting that their anti-German propaganda should not be very forceful.

2. Stefan Norblin, a famous painter of Continental repute, who arrived in India in transit to Brazil and has since been accepted by the Polish Consul General at Bombay on the list of sponsored evacuees, has been heard to say that the British soldier is a hopeless fighter, that the

British are bound to lose, and that the Japanese and the Germans will soon effect a juncture at India's northern frontiers. He is so panic-stricken that he has actually evacuated from Bombay and gone to live in Morvi state, as he feels that it would be safer in an Indian state. When he came to report his departure at this office he stated that he was going there to fulfil a contract in which he had to paint murals for the Maharajah. It was later ascertained that he has taken with him all his belongings, which fact belies his statement of going there on a temporary visit.

3. Stefan Bogucki arrived in transit to Brazil. He is now employed by the Polish Consul General at Bombay, and was, therefore, on his application, granted permission to reside in India while so employed. He is reported to have approached several refugees to include his name amongst any batch which may be arranging to leave India for a safer country.

Further, class and status were supposed to strengthen commitment. In colonial sociologese, these refugees had all held 'responsible' positions in Poland and the Special Branch official emphasized that he was therefore 'not quoting the mentality of the rabble'. Recommending further that such refugees be herded into a camp, he concurred with the foreign intelligence officer that this would 'act as *a stimulus to them to leave India*, to which there is no objection' (emphasis added).[27]

Refugees were also made to testify to the correctness of the testimony of other fellow refugees, as in the case of Chaim Szpilberg, employed at the Woollen Mills, Kanpur. He had to give a blow-by-blow account of the travels in refugee status of Abe Majzlisz, his companion from Horochow, Volhynia in Poland since 1930, through Lithuania, Japan, China and, finally, India.[28] Szpilberg's testimony itself, most ironically, reads like an interrogating officer's account of a criminal suspect. Detailed and self-vouching in its implication, the production of documents such as these must have only served to deepen still further the fear of behaving normally and the psychological implications of such a self-interrogating process cannot perhaps even be imagined.

The 'accommodating' side of the treatment meted out thus lay in the refugee's usability status. Erwin Reichenbaum and his wife Sarah

Goloschein, both Polish Jews, joined the King's Commission in the British Army and the Press Censor respectively within three months of their arrival in India in 1939 and they were being considered by 1945 for naturalization status.[29]

At times, disputes among the refugees themselves could lead to the creation of uncomfortable situations. One particularly notable case was that of a Polish consulate officer who, in 1943, threatened an impecunious couple, Mr and Mrs Domeszewicz, with sending them to a concentration camp back in Poland if they did not drop certain financial claims against his office.[30] Such disputes inevitably led to the involvement on one side or the other of the local police,[31] as it did in this instance, underlining more clearly the terms of refugee presence than the trivia of the disputes and foibles of every-day life.

## CONCLUSION

To recapitulate the two points that have been made in this paper: One, that in the period characteristically associated with Fascism in world history, a British xenophobia was rampant. This sentiment determined colonial attitudes even vis-à-vis Jewish and other refugees. However, this xenophobia came not from the exigencies of a political temporality located in the 1930s but, in fact, emerged from the imperial-colonial syndrome in which its first fractures were introduced by contemporary nationalisms in the First World War.

Second, and simply, neither entry into British India, nor the actual every-day life of European exiles, was easy. The standard dislocations associated with all forms of displaced life aside, the colonial Indian Government's handling of the problem between 1934 and 1945 was more an exercise in the management of pressures.[32] In dealing with a necessary evil, it was deeply conditioned by the mentality of exclusiveness. Least of all was it prompted by humanitarian concerns with which refugee questions are so deeply associated.

In asserting this second point a moral emphasis critical of colonial rule from a non-Indian nationalist point of view has deliberately been introduced. This is done to offset the moral tone of a historical analysis that is limited not only in its self-referentiality[33] (Fascism and its other) but equally in its implied assertions of what is supposed to have constituted the normative practices of abnormal and war-torn worlds. If such identities of association have remained hidden, they must now be ferreted out.

# NOTES

*A word of thanks*: The author wishes to thank Krittika Banerjee and Susan George but for whose help with documentation this paper could not have been written.

1. For the cross-weave of ideologies and mentalities in the imperial-colonial syndrome, see Mary Louise Pratt: *Imperial Eyes: Travel Writing and Transculturation*. London: 1992. The 'Indian' instance of this is best illustrated by Suhash Chakravarty, *The Raj Syndrome: A Study in Imperial Perceptions*, Delhi: 1991.
2. Otto Honigmann, Permission to visit Baltistan or Ladakh. Foreign Department, Frontier B Progs. nos. 1-2, November 1911, pp. 2, 7-8, National Archives of India (NAI).
3. Recommendation in favour of Dr Karl Wolfskehl and others. Foreign Department. Progs no. 139/143, February 1911, pp. 1, 5, NAI.
4. Chakravarty, op. cit.
5. Letter of Dr. F. Freyesleben, imperial and royal Consul General (Calcutta) for Austria-Hungary re Miss Wilma von Holbein-Holbeinsberg and Miss Jane Exle, Foreign Department, Intl. Progs. 99-102, February, 1911, NAI.
6. Dr. M. Taute's request endorsed, Foreign Department, Progs. no. 108/109, May 1911, NAI.
7. Letter facilitating Dr. Scherman's visit to Burma, Foreign Department, Intl. Part B, Progs. 131-7, December 1910, NAI.
8. Viceroy's wish visiting party be treated as very distinguished guests. Note of Mensdorff, Austro-Hungarian Embassy, 17 December 1909, Foreign Department Intl. B, Progs. no. 42/54, April 1910, p. 3, NAI.
9. Record referred to in note 2.
10. H. de Hanke, with several aliases, Foreign Department/Secret I /51/ October 1910, NAI.
11. Eric Hobsbawm, *Age of Extremes: The Short Twentieth Century 1914-1991*, London: 1994, pp. 28, 31.
12. 'German Influence in India', Foreign and Political Department (Secret), Intl. Progs. nos. 1-13, February, 1916, p. 9, NAI.
13. Ibid., pp. 9-10.
14. Foreign and Political Department, WAR B Progs., no. 298, p. 16 for Cardinal Gasparri's letter of 24 May 1918 and pp. 17-19 for Cardinal de Hartmann's letter of 4 May 1918, NAI.
15. 'In the Name of Humanity', appeal by the Council of German Jewry, London, and the Jewish Relief Association, Bombay, file no. 2797/34 B Class, Political and Service Department, Maharashtra State Archives, Bombay.

16. File loc. cit., notice 'Visas for India', Refugees, 31 March 1939, p. 123.
17. Travellers on *Conte Biancamano* at Bombay, 7 February 1939. file, loc. cit., p. 35.
18. Handwritten official note dated 13 February 1939, signature illegible, file, loc. cit., pp. 55-6, and GoI. Deputy Secretary to Chief Secretary, Bombay, 21 March 1939, p. 99.
19. Documents pertaining to Israel and Adele Minner, file, loc. cit., p. 151 and especially, Commissioner, Police, Bombay to Chief Secretary, Govt. of Bombay, 21 February 1940, pp. 179 f.
20. Circular, in file no. 127/39. Home Political, NAI.
21. Review of the cases of refugees, anti-Nazis, etc., External Affairs, GoI, 32(3) W of 1944, NAI.
22. Home Department Note of 16 January 1940 by C.J:W. Lillie, Home, Public, file no.10/130/39, p. 20, NAI.
23. Intelligence Bureau note of 29 January 1940, ibid., pp. 20-1. [Emphasis added.] At the risk of a brief digression, it may be speculated here that British ambivalence regarding who is good Aryan and who is a 'fallen' Aryan may well be the nineteenth-century colonial mentality informing this particular stance towards Jewish refugees. Such points are of course never 'proved', but for evidence of the manifestation of this attitude see Thomas Metcalf, *Ideologies of the Raj*, Delhi: 1995, p. 90.
24. Polish refugees as 'officially sponsored evacuees', V. Shankar, Deputy Secretary, GoI, to Consul General for Poland at Bombay, 27 May 1942, External Affairs file no. 276(4)-X 1942, pp. 27-8.
25. Bombay Special Branch to Intelligence Bureau, New Delhi, letter 20 March 1942, ibid., p. 17.
26. Ibid.
27. Ibid., pp. 17-18.
28. Testimony of Chaim Szpilberg, 25 June 1943, file no. 294(2)-X, External Affairs Department, 1942, p. 8, NAI.
29. From Captain Reichenbaum to the Secretary, GoI, Home Department, New Delhi, through the CO central internment camp, Dehra Dun, 14 April 1945, Home public file no.10/11/45, p.1, NAI.
30. The Case of Mons. Domeszewicz, External Affairs file no. 370-F/43, 1942, p. 37, NAI.
31. Ibid., p. 36.
32. An entirely comprehensive account of this exercise is historically documented by Joan Roland: *Jews in British India: Identity in a Colonial Era*, Hanover and London: 1989, pp. 211-37.
33. This would be my criticism of Roland's account, in sympathy with the argument of Robert Braun who disaggregates, 'The Holocaust and Problems of Historical Representation', in *History and Theory*, vol. 33, no. 2, 1994, pp. 173-97.

# Indian Responses to the Holocaust

*Tilak Raj Sareen*

The systematic mass murder of the Jews by the Nazis was an event of an unprecedented nature in the history of the world. Despite worldwide reaction against such genocide Nazi Germany continued its policy and no one altogether understood how this mass murder on such a large scale could have happened or could have been allowed to happen.[1] Historians are still debating this issue and no one has been able to deliver the final judgement. The massacre of so many innocent and defenceless people, doubtless in some profound sense, escapes understanding. Perhaps a thorough study of this event in a dispassionate manner by the historians is yet to be undertaken. Here I am not concerned with the historical or ideological background of this unfortunate event, but with the response in India during and after the war.

The Nazis' state-controlled anti-Semitism presented the world with a new challenge. The Indian national leaders, though too preoccupied with their struggle against the British, were emotionally genuinely moved by the sufferings of the Jews. But except frequent expressions of sympathy or horror against Nazi crimes, there was well-nigh nothing which these leaders could do to stop their extermination, though various solutions were proposed to mitigate their plight.

The rise of the Nazis initially threatened and eventually shattered the political order established by the promoters of the Versailles Treaty. The rise of Hitler and his policy towards the Jews began to appear in the Indian press too. The first outspoken condemnation was voiced by Pandit Jawaharlal Nehru, the leader of the Indian National Congress and the most outspoken critic of imperialism. The threat to the old order posed by Nazism became the dominant theme of his speeches and writings before and after the war.

'Few people', Nehru wrote, 'can withhold their deep sympathy from the Jews for the long centuries of most terrible oppression to which they have been subjected all over Europe. Fewer still can repress their indignation at the barbarities and racial suppression of Jews which the Nazis have indulged in, during the last few years and which continues today. Even outside Germany, Jews baiting has become a favourable pastime of various fascist groups.'

This revival 'in an intense form of racial intolerance and race war' was utterly repugnant to Nehru and deeply distressed him since many of these unfortunate people, with no country or home to call their own, were known to him, and some of them were friends.[2]

Like Nehru, Mahatama Gandhi, who was spearheading the struggle against the British, was equally concerned with the plight of the Jews though in a different way, and each tried to find a way out to ease their sufferings. It has been asserted, by many historians that Nazi goals for the Jews were formally set on emigration in the 1930s, when this procedure seemed to afford the most reasonable prospect of ridding the Reich from those held to be its most deadly enemies.[3] Nehru was a strong supporter of inviting the Jews to settle down in India despite opposition from many quarters. In his view this was the only way by which Jews could be saved from the wrath of the Nazis.

The All-India Congress Committee received many applications from those Jews who were desirous of seeking employment in India. Many recommendations came from the German Indian Society, the German Emergency Committee and other organizations then functioning in Europe. Dr Fialla from Prague specially requested Nehru to find employment opportunities for Jewish experts in Indian economic life. He wrote: 'I am conscious that your time is occupied with the settlement of questions of bigger importance for India than the problem of acquiring Jewish refugees experts, but I hope you will kindly consider this problem too.' He offered a number of suggestions and sent them to Nehru for a follow-up under the prevailing conditions in India.[4]

Dr Fialla's main plea was that, though the Indian leaders and newspapers had often expressed their sympathies for the persecuted Jews and had condemned their humiliation and spoliation, this was not deemed sufficient, neither for the interests of India itself nor for the solution of the urgent Jewish question. His contention was that by inviting Jewish experts India would also benefit. He pleaded:

> Is it possible for India to do its part in the solution of this question to its own profit? Would it not be clever to use the opportunity of getting people of the highest knowledge and industrial efficiency for the evolution of Indian national

economies? Surely these people expulsed [sic] from their homes and looking for the possibility of living a human-worthy life would do their best for the country giving them this possibility and treating them like their own nationals.[5]

But since the Jewish situation in Central Europe, especially Germany and Czechoslovakia, was getting worse day by day and the Jews were keen to emigrate hurriedly, Dr Fialla suggested that a special commission be sent to Central Europe to select the Jewish experts and an organizing committee be constituted for this purpose. He, no doubt, agreed that the selection of Jewish experts from Germany and Austria itself would be very difficult because many top-notch Jewish experts had already emigrated, and many others had been ruined morally and corporally apart from being psychologically tortured at German concentration camps. He suggested that 'the best pre-conditions for a successful selection of experts according to our informations [*sic*] should be in Prague, where many first-rate Jewish experts and industrialists have shifted from [the] Sudeten area occupied by the Germans'.[6]

This suggestion had its effect and it was because of the efforts of Nehru and the All-India Congress Committee that quite a large number of Jewish experts could come to India. In the words of a Jewish writer, India

proved to be a generous mother, not only to the Jews who came to live here permanently, but she opened her doors freely to those who sought refuge with her temporarily when they were driven out or could no longer endure the disabilities imposed on them in the countries in which they had dwelt. Hundreds of highly qualified German and East European Jews were given refuge in India and provided facilities for the exercise of their professions here.[7]

Nehru, of course, played a notable role in getting the Government of India to take in the Jews, even though he was at that time engaged in a vigorous struggle against the British. He also succeeded in persuading the reluctant Indian Medical Council to recognize Continental European medical qualifications which enabled many highly skilled refugee doctors to practise in India. Most of these Jews went on to estabilish very successful careers and some introduced new industries into the country. Between 1933 and the outbreak of war, Nehru was instrumental in obtaining entry for several German Jewish refugees into India. A number of professional people from this community settled in Bombay and Calcutta during this period.

There is no doubt that Nehru was genuinely interested in the settlement of Jews in India, and the All-India Congress Committee, after having received many applications from Jewish doctors, chemists, engineers and film-makers, sent them to the proper authorities. But because of opposition from many quarters, a large-scale emigration of the Jews to India could not be achieved. The reasons were explained by Nehru in his letter to Mrs Calman, a German Jewess settled in London. He wrote:

I need hardly assure you that the sufferings of the Jews in Germany have greatly shocked all people here. I wish we could help these unfortunate sufferers. To some extent I have been trying to do so. I have received scores of applications and I have sent the information to various provincial governments and industrialists. I understand that a number of Jewish refugees have already come to India, but I fear that it will become more and more difficult for others to come, as the difficulties placed in their way by the British Government are very great.[8]

Besides the opposition from the British Government, there were other reasons which prevented the Indian leaders from agreeing to the immigration of Jews on a large-scale into India. As Nehru explained:

It may, however, be possible for us to take some experts and specialists. But it is far more difficult for some thousands of men and women to be provided for in a separate colony or otherwise. This could only be done by setting apart agricultural land for the purpose. India, as you know, is a heavily populated country with a tremendous land hunger among the people, chiefly because the country is mainly agricultural. There are millions of unemployed on the land. It is one of our principal problems to find land for them or other occupations. It is difficult, in the face of this unemployment and land hunger, to set aside a large tract of territory for Jewish immigrants. But even apart from this, as I have said above, the governmental difficulties are almost insuperable. I am terribly sorry that we cannot do more than we are actually doing for the Jews. We know something of their being oppressed and persecuted and we are full of deep sympathy for the Jews in their distress. I am sure that in spite of everything, the Jews will overcome the obstacles and the difficulties which encompass them today.[9]

The Government of India, from the beginning, was opposed to the pro-Zionist policy of the Home Government. It was worried that such a policy would have an extremely bad effect on Indian Muslims. The Muslims in India were not only opposed to the settlement of Jews in India, but they also criticized the British policy of 'Jewish

Immigration into Palestine', which, in their view, was highly disastrous for the Arabs. In their propaganda in India, they apprehended that 'an undesirable type of Jew was getting into the country and that if immigration continued on its present scale, the Jews with their superior organisations and resources would tend to dispossess the Arabs of their property and place them in the position of permanent inferiority'.[10] With regard to the question of the settlement of the Jews, the policy of the Government of India was determined by its leanings towards the Muslims. Even before the war, the Foreign Office in London wanted the Government of India to help the Zionist organization functionary collect funds in India. The Viceroy was far from enthusiastic, and the Secretary of State for India, Lord Montague, though himself a Jew, was constrained to inform the Foreign Office about the 'expediency in the present state of Muslim opinion of forcing upon the attention of Indian Muhammadans a movement against which they are known to entertain some degree of resentment and suggested that the proposal be abandoned'.[11]

Quite understandably, the opposition to the Jews came from the Muslim leaders in India who were pro-Arabs. For them the bonds of religion were stronger than the sufferings of Jews under Hitler. Keeping in view the sentiments of the Muslims towards this question, the government imposed many restrictions on the settlement of Jews in India. How far the policy of the Indian National Congress to appease the Muslims was also responsible for this stand of the government needs further study. But there is no doubt that INC's pro-Palestinian policy encouraged the British to insist that each Jewish refugee have a guaranteed job before being allowed entry into India.

On the other hand, Mahatama Gandhi kept quiet on this question though his sympathies were with the Jews whom he had known during his South African days, and in his view, the 'German persecution of the Jews seems to have no parallel in History. The tyrants of old never went so mad as Hitler seems to have gone. And he is doing it with a religious zeal.'[12] He proposed that if there could be a justifiable war in the name of and for humanity, a war against Germany to prevent the wanton persecution of a whole race would be completely justified. Since he was against war, Gandhi's remedy of offering *satyagraha* was far from satisfactory and was considered unrealistic. He wrote:

If I were a Jew and were born in Germany and earned my livelihood there, I could claim Germany as my home even as the tallest German may, and challenge him to shoot me or cast me in the dungeon: I would refuse to be expelled or to submit to discriminating treatment and for doing this, I should not wait for the fellow Jews to join me in rival resistance but would have confidence that in the end the rest are bound to follow my example.

He was sure that if one Jew or all the Jews were to accept the above prescription, then, 'they cannot be worse off than now'. He asked the Jews to offer *satyagraha* as it was easier for them to do so since they were 'a compact, homogeneous community in Germany' and they 'have organised world opinion behind them'. He was convinced, he wrote further, 'that if someone with courage and vision can arise among them to lead them in non-violent action, the winter of their despair can in the twinkling of an eye be turned into the summer of hope'.[13] Gandhi was firmly convinced that if Hitlerism was to be destroyed, it would be destroyed only by non-violence.

This suggestion of Gandhi came in for a great deal of criticism, especially his view of advocating *satyagraha* which could not be applied in Germany. The editor of the *Jewish Frontier*, Hayim Greenberg, specially pointed out the impossibility of applying the technique of *satyagraha* in Germany. 'A Jewish Gandhi in Germany', he pointed out, 'should one arise, could function for about five minutes until the first Gestapo agent would lead him, not to the concentration camp, but directly to the guillotine.'[14]

Further, Gandhi's suggestion that the Western nations should go to war against Germany on account of the persecution of the Jews was not appreciated by the Jews themselves. The *Jewish Tribune* of Bombay considered it as a 'mischievous lie and must be nailed to the counter'. The Jews in India who had settled here had not been very vocal with regard to the happenings in Europe. They had, however, been very much interested in the Zionist movement and were in favour of a separate homeland for the Jews. They became articulate only when Gandhi wrote the above-mentioned article in the *Harijan*. The *Jewish Tribune* anticipated that in case of a war, the Jews would suffer more than the rest of the population. It pleaded that the 'Jew is a great lover and advocate of peace' and Gandhi was asked to 'refute any such allegation that is made against them'.

In the face of the foregoing weighty arguments, Gandhi withdrew his remarks about the advocacy of war for the sake of the Jews, and wished that 'somehow or other the persecution of Jews in Germany will end'.[15]

On the other hand, public opinion condemned outright Hitler and his policy towards the Jews. The nationalist press headed by the

*Hindustan Times* proposed the snapping of economic relations with Germany. The paper cautioned that 'the fate of German Jews should warn us what will befall us in the event of our establishing friendly relations with Germany. Germany has always tried to establish political domination over the countries brought under the economic control.'[16] The daily reports about the persecution of Jews in Germany resulted in the widespread boycott of German goods and German firms much to the embarrassment of German diplomats who were posted in India. However, there were some voices in favour of Germany's propagation of the theory of 'Aryan race'. Some portion of the Hindus did start imagining that the Germans were brothers under a skin, 'a comforting delusion for those smarting under the lash of colour prejudice'.[17] There were some groups, which were in favour of seeking help from Germany for India's liberation, though they were not in favour of Hitler's anti-Jewish policies. For example, Subhas Chandra Bose did seek help from Germany for India's liberation, though he never supported Hitler's racial policy.[18]

The war completely eclipsed the daily murder of the Jews under the official propaganda of 'evacuation or resettlement'. Though the American intelligence agencies knew of the 'Final Solution' with respect to the Jews from Germany, the Allied military authorities refused to bombard concentration camps on the ground that it would divert from the main war effort.

During the war, the Indian leaders had been put in prison for their activities against the British, so, naturally, like other nations, India also remained a passive witness to the fate of the Jews in Germany. Muslim as well as official attitude was largely determined by its policy towards Palestine. The sympathies of the Indian leaders no doubt were entirely on the side of the Arabs in their struggle, but, at the same time, they were not opposed to a separate homeland for the Jews. Like Winston Churchill and Albert Einstein, the Congress leaders did not believe that the settlement of Jews in Palestine would solve the Jewish problem. Moreover, they were apprehensive about British motives in dividing Palestine.

So far as the Jews in India were concerned, they were no doubt equally stirred by the fate of their brethren in Germany, but were not in a position to do anything positive or alleviate their sufferings. For them, the recognition of the 'national status of the Jewish people by the British Government and her allies' was one of the greatest event in the Jewish history and they were quick to leave for Israel when the state came into being in 1948 despite opposition from all sides.

It is surprising that the subject of Jews and their wholesale extermination has not attracted the attention of Indian historians. May be the events are yet shrouded in mystery or they are considered incomprehensibile, though the Nuremberg war crime trials brought to the surface the torture and medical experiments which were carried out on the Jewish prisoners by the Germans. But it is clear that the Indian leaders were firmly opposed to Nazism, and after its disappearance from Germany, Nehru wrote: 'I am firmly opposed to it now as I was even before. The mere fact that the Nazis have disappeared from Germany does not affect one's reactions. Nazism may crop up again in any country, other than Germany under some other name.'[19]

To conclude on the moral plane, India's deepest emotions were stirred by the Nazi persecution of the Jews. Sitting far away, the humanitarian sentiments expressed by many of its leaders could never be translated into concrete assistance save that of accommodating those who could escape from Germany.

## NOTES AND REFERENCES

1. See Michael R. Marrus, 'The History of the Holocaust: A Survey of Recent Literature', in *The Journal of Modern History*, Vol. 59, No. 1, March 1987, p. 114.
2. Jawaharlal Nehru, *Eighteen Months in India*, Allahabad: 1938, pp.133f.
3. Marrus, op. cit., p.125.
4. All-India Congress Committee Papers, file no. D. 42/1938. Nehru Memorial Museum and Library, New Delhi.
5. Ibid.
6. Ibid.
7. Benjamin J. Israel, *The Bene Israel of India*, Bombay: 1984, p. 49.
8. S. Gopal (ed.), *Selected Works of Jawaharlal Nehru*, Vol. 9, New Delhi: 1976, pp. 224f.
9. Ibid.
10. Home Department (Political), file no. 31/1/36, National Archives of India, New Delhi.
11. Foreign Department, file no. 171/1923, External Branch, National Archives of India, New Delhi.
12. *The Collected Works of Mahatma Gandhi*, Vol. 68, pp. 138f.
13. Ibid. For details on this controversy between Gandhi and the Jews of Germany for following the technique of *satyagraha*, see

Margaret Chatterjee, *Gandhi and his Jewish Friends*, London: 1992, pp. 115-22.

14. See Hayim Greenberg, 'We are Treated as Subhuman: We are Asked to be Superhuman', in *Harijan*, 27 May 1939, pp. 139f.
15. Ibid.
16. *The Hindustan Times*, Delhi, 26 May 1939.
17. Margaret Chatterjee, op. cit., p. 122.
18. For details see T.R. Sareen, *Subhas Chandra Bose and Nazi Germany*, Delhi: 1996.
19. S. Gopal (ed.), op. cit., Vol.14, p. 439.

# From Persecution to Freedom: Central European Jewish Refugees and their Jewish Host Communities in India

*Shalva Weil*

## INTRODUCTION[1]

The Central European Jews who reached India's hospitable shores in the 1930s and 1940s were not the first European Jews to reach India's soil; nor were they the first to maintain contact, however cursory, with other Indian Jewish communities. As early as 1738, the Dutch missionary J.A. Sartorius addressed a letter to Professor A.H. Francke of Halle referring to 'Indian and German Jews resident in Madras'. These Jews were acquainted with the Jews of Cochin on the Malabar coast, from whom they received information on a people in Surat and Rajapore who 'do not call themselves Jews, nor understand the name, but Bene-Israel, children or descendants of Israel' (Sartorius, 1858 in Fischel, 1972).[2]

In the nineteenth century, two Germans of Jewish descent visited India and met other German Jews there. The flamboyant missionary Reverened Joseph Wolff, whom Hugh Evan Hopkins entitles the 'sublime vagabond', was the son of a German rabbi who worked actively (and yet apparently with little success) in the 1830s to convert the Jews of India and elsewhere to Christianity (Hopkins, 1984). In the 1860s, a second German Christian missionary of Jewish descent Reverend J.M. Eppstein, also failed to convert Indian Jews to his religious persuasion. Nevertheless, in a record of the work of the London Society for Promoting Christianity from 1809 to 1908, Reverend W.T. Gidney does mention that, in Eppstein's case, 'amongst the Arab and the German Jews preaching of the Gospel has not been entirely without effect. Two from amongst the latter, both very intelligent young men, have lately been baptized in Bombay' (Gidney, 1908: pp. 384f.).

One can only speculate on what attracted Germans to India as early as the eighteenth century. Certainly, in those days, they did not flee to the Indian haven out of necessity, as they did later in our own century. The fascination of European and particularly German intellectuals with the nativist, ethnic romanticism, for India was strong and gave rise to conception of an Indo-Germanic culture, which, on the one hand, led to some of Europe's greatest artistic and philosophical achievements, but, in a bitter irony, led to the rationalization of some of its most cruel, even inexplicable, ideas. It is from the implementation of these ideas as deeds that some German Jews fled in the 1930s and 1940s and thereby reached India.

## PERSECUTION VERSUS TOLERANCE

A dialectic exists between the Jewish host communities in India and the Jewish emigrants who came to live in their midst in the 1930s and 1940s. While members of the former never suffered from anti-Semitism in any form in India,[3] most of the latter were escaping persecution resulting from a macabre racism. The contrast was incredible. In India, the Jews lived a comfortable existence, incorporated, as they were, into the hierarchical system of things. The Jews from Germany, certainly by the 1940s, had narrowly escaped one of the greatest tragedies of the modern world. They came to India, the most tolerant country in the world for Jews, but even there they had to find their place in a society where colour and caste determined the status of the individual and the community, and the British Government still regarded them as 'enemy aliens'.

In this paper, I shall describe the host Jewish communities and where, how, and if at all, the European Jewish refugees were incorporated. I shall examine the attitudes of the differing Jewish communities (and Indian society, in general) to the immigrants, the aid the local Jews offered the refugees and the causes with which the different groups worked together.

## THE JEWISH COMMUNITY INFRASTUCTURE IN THE 1930S AND 1940S

When the Central European Jews started arriving in India in the 1930s,[4] they came to a strange country with a foreign Jewish community infrastructure. In fact, there was no single community infrastructure *per se*, but a network of at least three established Jewish communities, which maintained complex relations among themselves. In addition, there were hundreds of other non-European Jews who were converging on India in the same period. Let me briefly describe the Jewish host communities, and then analyse the relationship between the new arrivals from Germany and these respective communities.

## THE BENE ISRAEL

The Bene Israel—their name means 'The Children of Israel' constituted the largest Indian Jewish community. According to their tradition, they were members of the Lost Tribes of Israel. The myth of their origin relates, that they were shipwrecked off the coast of India in the year 175 BC (cf. Kehimkar, 1937). They lost their holy book and only remembered the basic Jewish prayer, the *Shema*, in which Jews declare their faith in monotheism. The seven men and seven women who survived took refuge in the village of Nowgaow in the Konkan, where they buried the bodies of their relatives and friends who were washed ashore. Today, two mounds representing the graves of the shipwrecked males and females constitute proofs of these events in the eyes of Bene Israel (while, at the same time, explicating gender relations within the community) (Weil, 1996). In the course of time, the Bene Israel took up the occupation of oil-pressing and became known as *Shanwar Telis* or Saturday Oilmen because they refrained from work on Saturdays in accordance with the dictates of the Jewish religion.

The Bene Israel were not in contact with Jewry in the rest of the world until the advent of a visitor known as David Rahabi, who probably arrived in the eighteenth century.[5] From this time onwards, the Bene Israel began their gradual alignment with other Jews. Several factors contributed to this process. The British offered the Bene Israel, as a non-Hindu minority, educational and employment opportunities and they eventually moved out of the villages to Bombay and other cities. The Christian missionaries mentioned earlier, though having achieved little success in converting the Bene Israel, paradoxically, aided them to affiliate with other Jews by introducing them to the Hebrew Bible and other religious texts in Marathi translation. The Cochin Jews acted as cantors, ritual slaughterers and teachers for the Bene Israel, and the Baghdadi Jews who arrived in Bombay and

Calcutta, served as a reference model for normative Judaism.

The Indian Jewish population, the majority of whom were Bene Israel, increased from 6,000 in the 1930s to nearly 22,000 in 1941. I would like to point out here that these statistics were available to us, thanks to a German Jewish refugee namely H.G. Reissner. In a footnote to his article in the *Jewish Social Studies* Reissner states: 'The writer completed this study in 1948, after a nine years' stay in India. He wishes to express his thanks and appreciation to all his friends in India for their advice and co-operation' (Reissner, 1950: 349). Ironically, he provides no statistics on Jews of European origin in India.

## THE COCHIN JEWS

The settlement of Jews on the Malabar coast is fairly ancient and is mentioned in local Christian legends. According to one theory, the ancestors of today's Cochin Jews came to South India with King Solomon's merchants, who brought ivory, monkeys and parrots for the temples; words derived from Sanskrit and Tamil appear in *Kings I*. The most popular theory among the Jews is that they came to the Malabar coast some time in the first century AD.

Documentary evidence of Jewish settlement in south India can be found in the famous Cochin Jewish copper plates written in an ancient Tamil script. Until recently, the copper plates were dated 345 AD, but contemporary scholars agree upon the date 1000 AD. In that year, during the reign of Bhaskara Ravi Varman (962-1020), the Jews were granted seventy-two privileges, some of which are as follows: the right to use a day lamp, the right to blow a trumpet and exemption from particular taxes. The privileges were bestowed upon the Cochin Jewish leader Joseph Rabban, 'the proprietor of the *Anjuvannam*,[6] [and on] his male and female issues, nephews and sons-in-law'.

The Cochin Jews were divided into White and Black Jews, the two groups neither intermarrying nor interdining. The Black Jews claim that they are the original recipients of the copper plates, thereby proving their high status in the South Indian context. However, the copper plates are today in the hands of the White Jews of Spanish, Portuguese, Iraqi, Yemenite and European origin, many of whom arrived on the Malabar coast from the sixteenth century onwards.

In 1947, the Cochin Jews, the smallest Jewish community in the world, numbered 2400 souls (Reissner, 1950). In 1953-4, nearly the whole community went to live in Israel. Today, only a handful of Jews remain on the Malabar coast.

## THE BAGHDADI JEWS

The group colloquially called the 'Baghdadis' came largely from Iraq (but also from Syria and other places) from the end of the eighteenth century onwards to two major centres: Bombay and Calcutta. The first settlers were Shlomo Cohen (1762-1836) who reached Calcutta in 1798 and and Suleiman ibn Yaqub (also known as Solomon Jacob) (1795-1833), who worked at the turn of the century in Bombay (Ezra, 1986). They dealt in the gem trade, rose water and the import of Arabian horses, cotton and opium. Two prominent dynasties were the House of David Sassoon (1792-1865) in Bombay and the Ezra family in Calcutta. The merchant princes provided employment for approximately 5,000 'Baghdadis', who worked in the mills and multifold enterprises as workers, clerks or brokers. The upper-class Baghdadis tended to run the synagogues and set up charitable institutions for the poor.

The 'Baghdadis' identified themselves with the British elites and maintained direct contact with England and British educational and cultural institutions. When Indian independence came, most of them opted to move to England, Australia and other English-speaking countries. Approximately 400 'Baghdadis' remain in India today in Bombay and Calcutta.

## THE EASTERN JEWISH REFUGEES

In addition to the three established Jewish communities in India in the 1930s and 1940s, each with its own synagogue and communal organizations and particular rituals and customs and special songs, there were other Jews who reached India, if temporarily during these very years.

During the 1930s and 1940s, hundreds of Eastern Jews fled their countries such as Persia, Bukhara and Afghanistan and came to India. In Afghanistan, for example, after the assassination of Mohammed Nadir Shah in 1933, the ruler who had protected the Jews in that country, hundreds of Jews fled for their lives to India. They were joined by Bukharan Jews and Jews from Persia. The Indian Goverment extended visas for these refugees, but demanded guarantees (from the Afghani Government and others) that they were not Bolshevik agents. Most of this group of Jews regarded their stay in India as transitory, as a footstep to reach Palestine; only a few wanted to remain in India. In a recent article by G. Pozialov, the wanderings of some of these refugees from one Asian country to another have been described from the 1930s to the 1950s (Pozialov, 1994). The refugees suffered from Soviet emigration restrictions, on the one hand, and immigration restrictions on the part of the British Government, on the other. In addition, Pozialov points out that the Zionist leadership in Palestine perceived European immigration as a greater priority.

During their transitory stay in India, these Eastern Jews did not establish their own synagogues or community facilities, but naturally joined the 'Baghdadi' community in religious worship. Although they did not constitute an Indian Jewish community *per se*, their existence in India is important since our focus is European Jewish immigrants and their relations with the Jews they found in India during this period.

## INTERACTIONS AMONG THE HOST JEWISH COMMUNITIES

### *Complex Relationships*

Relationships among the different Jewish communities in India were complex from the beginning and especially so in the 1930s and 1940s, as new groups, such as the European and the Oriental Jewish refugees, came on the scene.

Of course, there was a vast distance between Cochin and Bombay, the centres of Jewish life in India, but, nevertheless limited contact did exist between the Cochin Jews on the one hand and the Bene Israel and the 'Baghdadis' on the other. Several Cochin Jews from the Black community served as religious functionaries in the Bene Israel community. In the 1930s there was even a stream of Cochin Jews—Black and White alike—who came to pray in the Bene Israel synagogues and a few even got married there.[7] Intermarriages between Black Cochin Jews and the Bene Israel were rare; I do not know of a single case of a member of the White Jewish community marrying a Bene Israel. The White Jews, on the other hand, did enter into marriage relationships with 'Baghdadi' Jews and even actively sought marriage partners among their ranks.[8]

The relationship of the Bene Israel with the 'Baghdadi' community is one of the primary concerns of at least one major study on Indian Jewry (Strizower, 1971). On the one hand, the 'Baghdadi' Jews extended assistance to the Bene Israel and many of the latter found work in the Sassoon Mills and other 'Baghdadi' enterprises. On the other hand, relations between the two communities were strained and both maintained a distance between each other. Marriages between the two communities were frowned upon, on both sides. Social contacts were restricted. Members of the Bene Israel community never prayed in the 'Baghdadi' synagogue and vice versa. The major reason for this was that the 'Baghdadis' did not really consider the Bene Israel as Jews and did not feel they could call upon them to count in a *minyan* (quorum).

### *Alliances*

Despite the differences among the Jewish communities, which centred around questions of status and religious observance, alignments certainly took place. From an analytical point of view, they focused around wider international issues, which crossed the parochial divisions of community.

### *Indian Nationalism*

In 1930 there was an attempt to form an Indian Jewish Nationalist Party, which would go beyond the petty divisions among the different Jewish communities. The party was led by Dr Abraham Erulkar, a Bene Israel doctor,[9] and a fierce Indian nationalist; he was the vice-president of the Home Rule League. About 75 people, mostly of Bene Israel origin, attended a meeting at which he presided, but one 'Baghdadi' observed that although his people sympathized with the cause, they could not openly support the movement because they were employed in the Sassoon Mills (and the Sassoons, it will be recalled, were close to the British) (Roland, 1989, p. 104).

### *Zionism*

Throughout the 1930s the Jewish agency attempted to broaden the base of the Zionist movement to include the Jews of India. This agency sent out a number of emissaries from Palestine, the most famous of whom was Dr E. Olswanger, a Sanskrit expert.[10]

In 1931, there was a call for all three Indian Jewish communities to unite to form the Indian Zionist Federation, but tensions developed among the different groups. Meanwhile, different Zionist institutions established branches in India. In 1936, the Keren Kayemet and the Keren Hayesod, two organizations which raised money for the Zionist movement, agreed in principle to work in India; in 1935 the youth group Habonim set up an experimental farm in Bombay; in 1937 the Bombay Zionist Association (BZA), founded in 1920, was transferred to permanent premises in Bombay; in 1938 WIZO (Women's International Zionist Organization) established à Bombay Branch in the same year (Weil 1982, 174). Two Zionist newspapers, the *Jewish Advocate* and the *Jewish Tribune* were published and distributed from Bombay.

## THE CENTRAL EUROPEAN JEWS: SKETCHING A PROFILE

Against the foregoing complex backdrop, Central European Jews along with other European gentiles began to arrive in India from the 1930s onwards. Some emigrated by choice, sometimes lured by the attractions of Hinduism or India; others came to escape the rise of Fascism. By the end of the 1930s and in the 1940s, they arrived in India, fleeing from the nightmares of the holocaust.

Before I discuss the relationship between the refugees and the host Jewish communities, let me attempt to sketch a profile of these people in India. In order to provide a complete profile, it should be possible in theory to obtain from the archives the names of all the European Jews who arrived in India in the 1930s and 1940s and trace where they eventually settled and what happened to them; it is certain that a number of them could be traced in Israel. An even more ambitious task would be to sketch a social profile of every single emigré, by conducting in-depth interviews with those who are still alive. In the absence of such research, let me point to general indicators.

### *Countries of Origin*

Many of the emigrants/refugees came from Germany and Austria. There were also refugees from Hungary, Czechoslovakia, Poland and Romania.

### *Numbers*

How many Central European Jews are we talking about? In the 1930s the numbers were small but sufficient to set up the Jewish Relief Association (JRA) by 1934 in Bombay, with branches, established later, in Calcutta and Madras. The association was due to be 'a purely charitable association to assist European Jews who found their way to hospitable India but had no means of livelihood, as in most cases they were victims of racial persecution'. At the outbreak of the war, the JRA had helped provide 1000 refugees with visas. In 1941, the Jewish Agency archives tell of 700 refugees from Austria and Germany in India. I. Cowen mentions 1300 refugees from Europe who reached India (Cowen, 1971). In 1943, the JRA published the figures of 'Continental Jews' which totalled 1080 (*Jewish Advocate*, July 1943).

It should be pointed out that not all emigrés or refugees were in touch with the JRA, although by 1939 there was an agreement between the Council of German Jewry, which backed the JRA, and the India Office of the British Government, that the decision regarding entry would be taken together. The ultimate authority would rest with the Goverment of India, whereas the JRA would have to provide guarantees for the refugees for five years. It is possible that until 1939 several hundred refugees slipped through the fingers of the JRA. After the Second World War, so many refugees and displaced persons were arriving for brief periods in India that not all of them may have been recorded. Therefore, a cautious estimate of the number of Central European Jews who reached India during the 1930s and 1940s including those who were only in India for short stays, would certainly exceed 2000 souls; the exact number still has to be ascertained.

### *Educational and Occupational Levels*

Many of the Central European Jews in India were quite highly educated and included in their ranks a large number of doctors. Amongst the 1080 refugees maintained in the JRA 1943 records, 25 were aged and unemployed; 350 were women and children[11] 147 were interned in camps or parole centres, 225 were in 'commercial employment' or employed as clerks, 58 were merchants, 110 were technicians or employed in the war production, 20 were manufacturers of government orders, 127 were doctors or dentists of whom 29 were employed in the Royal Army Medical Corps, and 11 served as civil MDs in military hospitals. Those who were unemployed and living in hostels numbered 18. It appears that there were additional doctors and others who were not listed in the JRA records.

## RELIGIOUS AND COMMUNAL DISPOSITIONS

Analytically, the Central European Jews can be divided into three groups, according to the extent of their religious/communal affiliation.

The first group consisted of Jews (or part-Jews) who came to India because of the lure of its culture, mysticism or politics. Some of these Jews emigrated to India by choice, even before they realized that Fascism was on the rise in Europe. Included in this group were a few Jews who adopted Hinduism, including a Jewish pianist from Vienna, whom Alfred Wuerfel, a former officer in the German Consulate, met in Benares in 1939. He became known as 'Atmananda'. Another Jew, Walter Eidlitz, a writer from Vienna and married to a Swedish lady, with whom Wuerfel became acquainted at the Dehra Dun Internment Camp, also had been converted to Hinduism by a German Swami (personal correspondence 15 May 1995).[12] Others were lured by the political philosophy of Mahatma Gandhi, for instance, Margarete Spiegel who stayed with him as a disciple for a year in his first *ashram* at Sabarmati.

Some emigrés/refugees found themselves attracted by Indian culture once they had arrived in India and contributed enormously to the flourishing of its cultural life (cf. Voigt, 1991). An excellent example was Rudolf von Leyden, the art critic of the *Times of India*. It is still not clear what motivated Rudolf and Albrecht von Leyden to come to India (Anna Winterberg, personal correspondence 8 August 95), but they were no doubt pinpointed as people of Jewish descent in the increasingly racist climate prevalent in Nazi Germany in the 1930s. The irony was that Rudolf von Leyden's grandfather was not Jewish, although his grandmother was and her name was Oppenheim (Winterberg, op. cit.), but that von Leyden, and many others who came to India, represented what the philosopher I. Deutscher has so poignantly termed as the 'non-Jewish Jew' (Deutsher 1968). Needless to say, this group of 'non-Jewish Jews' had no affiliation with the established Jewish communities in India.

The second group consisted of orthodox and afflilating Jews who took an active part in synagogue services and Jewish community life. A good example would be Max Friedlander, currently living in the town of Ranaana in Israel, who established a commodities company initially in Calcutta and later in New York. Friedlander was an observant Jew, who regularly attended prayers in the vibrant Calcutta Jewish synagogue of those days and was an active community member.

The third group represented the bulk of the refugees, who received the assistance of the JRA and its guarantees in order to stay in India. These Jews frequented Jewish communal organizations, particularly at the beginning of their stay in India when they arrived as destitutes, but, with time, they gradually moved on and links with the Jewish community slackened. Most of these Jews requested for a transfer to Palestine; after the war, they departed for other countries, too.

## ATTITUDES TOWARDS CENTRAL EUROPEAN EMIGRANTS/ REFUGEES IN INDIAN SOCIETY

The vast majority of Indians was totally unaware that large groups of people, mainly Jews from Europe, were seeking refuge on their shores. Nevertheless, the reactions to their arrival in certain (upper/middle-class) circles were out of proportion compared to the minuscule numbers they represented. The brunt of the reactions focused upon two major occupational groups, namely the businessmen and doctors.

### *The Businessmen*

Some businessmen arrived in India in the 1930s or even earlier in order to set up international enterprises. A good example is Gerhard Gabriel who left Germany in 1927 and arrived in India in 1929. Representing a German-Jewish import-export firm, he started his own company dealing in non-ferrous metals in Bombay in 1933. Another example was Bolek Rembaum from Poland, who set up an international business in Calcutta. His neighbour was the aforementioned Max Friedlander.

Businessmen who were already well entrenched in India were later joined by their family,[13] traders and other businessmen who fled from the holocaust and found themselves, sometimes not by design, in India. By 1943, some of the refugees had opened factories and were manufacturing goods and garments hitherto unknown in India; some of the manufacturers established international businesses.

The success of some of these refugees brought with it jealousy or even anti-Semitism. J.M.B. Gibbon, the president of the Bombay Chamber of Commerce, stated in 1943: 'Since India threw open her hospitable shores to the many unfortunates [who] were driven by the invader from their homes, there has sprung up especially in Bombay, a whole tribe of traders whose activities have been most unwelcome' (*Jewish Advocate*, 12 July 1943, p. 4).

### *The Doctors*

As early as 1934, there was already a public outcry against the large numbers of German doctors arriving in India, who were flooding

Bombay 'to the great detriment of that already grossly overcrowded profession'. In this context Captain Thornton wrote to the All-India Medical Council demanding at least legislation against German doctors. Presumably most, if not all of these doctors were Jews. The *Bombay Chronicle* published an article stating that a few Jewish physicians, if given refuge from Nazi persecution in Bombay, would not harm the medical profession. Likewise, the *Bombay Sentinel* reported that '. . . the medical fraternity in Bombay refused to countenance a ban on the Jewish doctors who sought refuge in Bombay . . . and will follow the ancient Indian traditions of affording shelter from persecution.'

According to Roland, there were *less than* 10 German doctors who had established practices in Bombay during this period, but they had proved themselves to be such successes that other doctors felt threatened (Roland, 1989, pp. 179ff.). By 1939 there were apparently only 42 refugee doctors in India (Roland, op. cit.), but antagonism continued. Manu Subedar, representing the Indian Merchants' Chamber, asked the government whether it might be considered desirable to transport some of the German doctors back to their homeland. One of the most interesting reactions came from Dr Abraham Erulkar, the Bene Israel nationalist referred to earlier. He pointed out that it was true that there might be too many doctors in the cities, but there was scope for the German doctors in the small towns and villages (Roland, op. cit.).

To summarize it can be said that most Indians were simply ignorant of the arrival of hundreds of Jews to India before and during the Second World War. Although the subject has still to be researched, Indian leaders did not effectively condemn the internment of German, Austrian and other nationals, including Jews from these countries by the British Government after the outbreak of war on 3 September 1939.

It seems obvious that those Jewish people who had been suffering in concentration camps like the one at Dachau and were still to face extermination camps like those of Auschwitz could hardly be expected to pose a threat to the British as supporters of the Nazi regime; nor could that be the case with other non-Jewish Europeans who had been living in India for several years and who had perhaps come to India in order to escape the rise of Fascism. But the general attitude was one of apathy.

## INTERFACE BETWEEN THE GERMAN JEWS AND THE JEWISH HOST COMMUNITIES

Although most of the European Jews came to India as a result of the persecution on the basis of religion and race, the irony was that for many of them, as we have noted earlier, as for much of European Jewry, their religion and race were of secondary importance to other modes of identification, such as their professional identity. Many of the immigrants had intermarried with members of other faiths in Europe.[14] Therefore, many of the refugees from an assimilated background did not make automatic contact with the local Jewish communities; they may have been unaware of the existence of Jews or organized Jewish communities in India. Nevertheless, interactions did take place, particularly with the 'Baghdadi' community. These interactions intensified as European Jews discerned the hope of a homeland of their own—in Palestine—and worked with the local Jewish communities to realize that hope. Before we turn to the issue of Zionism, let me make a brief survey of the Central European Jews' relations with the three major Jewish communities.

### *Relations with the Cochin Jews*

The Central European Jews tended to arrive mostly in Bombay and Calcutta and had litle connection with Cochin Jewry, which was quite some distance away. Nevertheless, one or two Jews reached the south. One of them, Hilda Elsberg, received employment in the Presentation Convent in Kodaikanal (Madras Presidency) as a dance and gym teacher. One or two others joined the Jewish community temporarily during the war years. In 1939, S.S. Koder, leader of the 'Paradesi' community and representative of the Cochin Jews in the Legislative Council, reportedly requested from the Dewan, Sir R.K. Sanmukham Chetty, permission to settle 250 Jewish families, but it is uncertain as to what became of this scheme (*Jewish Advocate*, 10 May 1939).

### *Relations with the Bene Israel*

There was little formalized contact between the Bene Israel communities and the Central European Jews in the cities where the former ran synagogues and prayer halls, e.g. in Bombay, Poona, Ahmedabad, New Delhi and Karachi (before partition). A review of the committee members of some Bene Israel synagogues during the 1930s and 1940s does not reveal any European or even non-Bene Israel names. Even the Jewish Religious Union synagogue, an affiliate of the Jewish Liberal Movement, which was founded by Lady Montague in 1925 and frequented by the elite of the Bene Israel, was neither attended by the German Jews, nor by the 'Baghdadis', who only began coming to services in the early 1950s after the community was headed temporarily by a dynamic British rabbi (of German origin).

Relations were, however, established between individuals. For instance, Sarah Israel, a member of the Bene Israel, recalls a family friendship with Dr Fred Tauber, a dentist, and his wife in Bombay. G.L. Gabriel, the aforementioned German Jewish emigrant, opened an alloy factory in partnership with a Bene Israel, Alex Elijah of Poona (although it should be noted that even Gabriel usually prayed in the 'Baghdadi' synagogue in Bombay). In addition, European doctors tended to members of the Bene Israel community, occasionally not demanding any payment.

Relations between the Bene Israel and the refugees (and emigrants) can be best expressed in the words of Sarah Israel: 'The main contact which we had with the refugee Jewish people who came to India was on a "personal" basis rather than a "community" basis' (personal correspondence 16 May 1995).

*Relations with the Baghdadis*

The European Jews, if and when they did affiliate themselves with a Jewish community, preferred to associate with the higher class or more Anglicized 'Baghdadi' Jews. Sometimes the aristocratic Ezra or Sassoon families mingled with the educated refugees. In a photograph I have discovered taken during a wedding at the Magen David synagogue in Calcutta dating to the late 1930s or early 1940s, the bride and groom, Dr and Mrs (Kupferstein), are flanked by Lady Ezra, of the prestigious 'Baghdadi' Ezra family, and Reverend Margulies, a chaplain in the British army. Also in the picture are Dr Gubbay, the daughter of Elias Joseph Ezra and other German refugees: Mr and Mrs Greenbaum and their daughter Ilse and Ms Hilda Friedlander.[15]

The more affluent German Jews, though often considering themselves superior to the 'Baghdadis', sometimes aligned with the latter when it came to business deals and frequented the same British clubs. In 1938, the Jewish club was opened in the Fort area in Bombay attracting 'Baghdadi' Jews and Europeans.[16]

In Bombay, the European Jews tended to attend the Knesset Eliahu synagogue which was situated in the Fort business area, but on the High holidays, Rosh Hashana and Yom Kippur, when more people would attend the synagogue they rented their own prayer hall. According to the *Jewish Tribune* (Vol. 8, 8 October 1937), some of the European Jews presumably the poorer ones, decided to move over to the 'Baghdadi' Magen David synagogue in the Byculla area of Bombay after the Knesset Eliahu synagogue started charging for seats.

Another interesting sidelight is that in the 'Baghdadi' Jewish cemetery in Bombay, there are over twenty graves of European Jews who were buried there in a special plot.[17] But, clearly, the poorer refugees naturally frequented the 'Baghdadi' institutions in the hope of receiving charity from members of the wealthy Sassoon dynasty and other families.

## COOPERATION WITH INDIAN JEWS ON A DAY-TO-DAY BASIS

There were two issues around which the Central European Jews worked hand in hand with members of all three existing Jewish communities in India, particularly with 'Baghdadis'. These issues were: refugee relief, and Zionism. It should be noted that excepting the unusual case of Margarete Spiegel, the German Jews never became involved in the Indian nationalist cause, from which they felt distanced, despite Gandhi's well-known personal friendships with Jews of German origin (e.g. Kallenbach). In addition, it should be mentioned as an exception to prove the rule that the well known communist leader M.N. Roy married one of European refugees being studied here.

I shall now only deal briefly with both the foregoing issues and touch upon isolated points; it is certainly not my intention to survey here the history of Zionism in India.

### *Refugee Relief*

As mentioned earlier, the JRA was established as early as 1934 to assist refugees. On the JRA board were prominent German Jews, as well as 'Baghdadi' Jews, who worked together for over a decade to raise funds for destitute immigrants and helping them financially and professionally. By 1942, the JRA had 300 members from across India. Its annual budget was Rs. 30,000 to 40,000 of which Rs. 12,000 to 15,000 were paid by refugees who had already established themselves with the aid of the association (*Jewish Advocate*, 12 October 1942). This also indicated something about the self-help nature of the refugees themselves.

The ambit of work of the JRA was enormous and admirable. The older, established refugees together with several local 'Baghdadi' Jews managed to save hundreds of souls. The iocal Jews would vouch for the immigrants claiming that they were essential for maintaining their enterprises in India or that they had indispensable occupations. Such was the case of Dr Leon Blum, a German doctor, who arrived on the Italian ship *Conte Rosso* in 1938 which had set sail from Genoa *en route* for Shanghai. The boat docked at Bombay and Dr Blum and his wife, Elizabeth, were taken to the residence of Edward Eini, a 'Baghdadi' Jew, who had guaranteed their stay in Bombay, without, of course, knowing them personally. After a few weeks, Eini paid for Leon and Elizabeth Blum to go to Poona, where they were placed in the hands of another member of the 'Baghdadi' community, Meyer. Dr Blum worked in Poona in the first Western-style hospital in India built by David Sassoon, the leader of the 'Baghdadi' community. Dr Blum left India some time after the Second World War; only further research will discover his destination.

*Zionism*

Sometimes the Zionist movement worked parallel to the rescue operations, and often Zionist organizations were manned by the same Central European and 'Baghdadi' Jews who led the refugee relief programmes (Fred Klein, for example, was chairman of the JRA and a member of the Palestine Office for India Committee). At times, however, there were tensions between the two objectives, which appeared contradictory: settlement in India, on the one hand, and repatriation to Palestine, on the other.

In 1939, when the Jewish Agency sent out Nedivi, the town clerk of Tel-Aviv as a Zionist emissary for 13 days, he met A. Shohet, a 'Baghdadi' Jew and editor of the *Jewish Advocate*, who told his readers that Indian Jews could understand how difficult the struggle was in Palestine if one could judge from 'how difficult it is to give shelter and work to only a handful of refugees'. In addition, he held talks with Nehru and Gandhi regarding the Zionist cause. Nedivi came to the conclusion after his visit, that in Zionist matters, one could only rely on a 'Baghdadi Jew' J.J. Gubbay and a German Jewish lady, Erna Petzal whose husband was a doctor. The other German Jews, A. Leiser and Fred Klein, he complained, were too busy with refugee affairs! (Central Zionist Archives, 51456). However, by the time Dr S. Lowy (a German Jew), visited India as a Zionist emissary later in 1939, Erna's husband, Dr Petzal, had been interned and Erna had been forced to give up her Zionist activity.

The tension between Zionism and refugee causes mounted. The Zionists felt that the rich local Jews like the Sassoons were being 'milked' by the refugee assistance committee at the expense of the contributions they used to make to the Zionist cause.

In the same year, i.e. 1939, Peter Krieger, a Hebrew teacher, who had been an active Zionist leader among Jewish youth in Germany and went to live in Palestine, was sent with his wife to Calcutta to teach Hebrew there for three years. In an epistle to the head of the Asian desk in the Jewish agency in 1941, Krieger described the general apathy towards Zionism. He wrote: 'as far as more active and wider Zionist activity among Indian Jewry is concerned, one has to take into consideration the degenerate cultural and spiritual situation of this Jewry. The communities are in no way organised, they have no rabbi, no culture and no interest.' The same impression is gained from a letter to Palestine (to Mr Epstein) written by yet another German Jewess, Dr Olga Feinbergy, a Calcutta Wizo member.

As the situation in Europe deteriorated and the Britisth Government severely limited entry visas into India, the position of the Central European Jews became desperate, particularly after the war began. A copy of a telegram I discovered in the Central Zionist Archives in Jerusalem sent from Bombay on 19 December 1945 and received in Jerusalem on 20 January 1946 reads as follows:

35 Jewish refugees mostly from Germany and Austria still restricted at Parole camps India threatened with compulsory repatriation to countries origin which they emphatically oppose stop Government might agree release for immigration Palestine stop To save them from repatriation please cable whether you prepared allocate 50 certificates near future for this pressing purpose. Matter most urgent. Palestine Office (S 63794).

By 1946, Central European Jews were vying with Jews from Persia, Afghanistan and other countries to get to Palestine. On 7 August 1946, H. Cynowicz, head of the Palestine Office for India, despatched 5 persons to Palestine: 3 were Afghan refugees, and 2 were refugees from the Polish camp at Kolhapur (now in Maharashtra). In an epistle to the Jewish Agency for Palestine, Cynowicz explains that although the five certificates received from Palestine were earmarked for Afghan

Jews, he included Mrs Tamba Drimer and her sons, Polish refugees, who had been in Kolhapur since 1943. By 1946 their case had become 'acute' since the Kolhapur camp was due to be closed imminently and they had nowhere to go; they had also been denied the right to stay in India. In an earlier document in the Central Zionist Archives dated 1 April 1946, Drimer was included in a list of 62 refugees demanding immigration visas for Palestine (S 63794). Tamba Drimer (no. 36) was described as follows: 'Age 42. Was evacuated with her husband and 5 children in 1940 to Russia. In 1941 she lost her husband and 3 children and has no information of them up to date. In 1942 she was evacuated with her two children [Leon Drimer no. 37 and Jacob Drimer no. 38] . . . to Iran and afterward to India where she is staying in the Polish Camp [of Kolhapur].

The only solution was a Jewish homeland to accommodate all the displaced persons who had reached India and other destinations after the Second World War.

## CONCLUSION

This paper has dwelt upon the relations between the Central European Jews who reached India during the 1930s and 1940s and the Jewish host communities. I pointed out that three separate Jewish communities existed in India, each with its own history and own traditions. Interactions among these Jewish communities were complex, influenced by considerations of distance from the centre and religious tradition. During the 1930s and 1940s the relationships among the communities were complicated even more by the influx of European Jews, on the one hand, and Oriental Jewish refugees from Persia, Bukhara and Afghanistan, on the other. India became the stage for playing out some of the dramatic events of the greatest modern tragedy that has befallen mankind: the Holocaust.

Interactions between the Central European Jews and the local Jewish communities were of differing natures depending upon the specific Jewish community and the status of the individuals. The Europeans tended to have personal relationships with a handful of elite Bene Israel, but the major contacts were with the 'Baghdadi' community, with whom they worked hand in hand for two causes: refugee relief and Zionism. After the Second World War, many of the European Jews left India for Palestine and other destinations.

The Central European Jews in India belonged sociologically to three groups: those who assimilated to Indian life, those who affiliated themselves strongly with the (Baghdadi) Jewish community and those who were dependent upon Indian Jewish assistance. Some members of the former two groups stayed on in India and became part and parcel of Indian or Indian Jewish life. The latter tended to regard India as a stepping-stone to permanent freedom.

## NOTES

1. I am grateful to the organizers of the seminar on Central European Jewish Emigration to India, 1933-45, for affording me the opportunity to participate, in particular, to Dr Georg Lechner for goading me into researching in greater detail the subject matter of this paper.
2. It should be noted that Sartorius refers to the Bene Israel, not in the Konkan villages or in Bombay, but in Surat and Rajapore.
3. The only time there was persecution against India's Jews was during the Portuguese invasion of South India in the sixteenth century (cf. Segal, 1993).
4. Not all the European Jews who arrived in India in the 1930s fled from the threat of Fascism; some came of their own free will seeking adventure, business opportunities or new horizons.
5. The exact identity of David Rahabi is unknown. Most likely he hailed from the family of the Cochin Jew, Ezekiel Rahabi, the Dutch East India Company's principal merchant in Malabar in the eighteenth century.
6. *Anjuvannam* is a source of controversy; it can refer to a kingdom, a place, an artisan class, a trade centre or a specifically Jewish guild (cf. Weil, 1986).
7. Two of the most famous 'Cochin' marriages which took place in Bene Israel synagogues in Bombay were that of A.B. Salem's son Balfour who married 'Baby' Koder, a member of the White Jews community. Salem was an educated *meshuchrar* (manumitted slave) who protested his inferior status. The marriage was prohibited in Cochin because it crossed subtle quasi-caste lines. A second Salem son was also forced to marry in Bombay. However, by 1979, the divisions between the White Jews and the *meshuchrarim* had broken down and another son of Salem married a member of the White community in a ceremony in the Paradesi synagogue, belonging to the White Jews, in Cochin itself.
8. In part 3, 'Leaves from a Family Tree', in E.D. Ezra's book *Turning Back the Pages: A Chronicle of Calcutta Jewry* (1986), there are a number of (White) Cochin 'Baghdadi' marriages recorded.
9. In July 1933, Dr Erulkar attended to Gandhi as President of the Indian Medical Council during his renowned 21day fast.

10. It was Dr E. Olswanger who published H.S. Kehimkar's important 1897 manuscript on the history of the Bene Israel as a book in Tel-Aviv (Kehimkar, 1937).
11. Apparently, unemployed.
12. I am grateful to Alfred Wuerfel for the rich information he has provided. Wuerfel himself arrived in India in 1935 to study Sanskrit at the Banaras Hindu University, where he stayed until the outbreak of the Second World War. On 3 September 1939, he was interned by the British Government and taken to Ahmednagar now in Maharashtra. After the war, Wuerful lived in Bombay where he became acquainted with educated Jewish refugees.
13. Gabriel's sister and husband joined him in 1933; his parents reached Bombay in 1938. In 1945, Gabriel married Vera Lewin, a Jewish refugee who arrived in Bombay in 1940. Information on Gabriel is taken from a pamphlet published on the occasion of a 'Felicitaion Meeting' on his eightieth birthday in 1987 at the auditorium of the ORT India Girls' School, Bombay.
14. To name but two out of the hundreds of examples, Willy Haas, the editor of the Cultural Section of *Die Welt*, who was born in Prague, represented an assimilated Jew; Walter Eidlitz, mentioned earlier had married a non-Jew.
15. I have received a photocopy of this wedding photograph from David and Isaac Sassoon, Jerusalem.
16. Today the same club is predominantly frequented by Bene Israel.
17. This information was reported to me by the keeper of the Jewish cemetery in Bombay, February 1994.

## REFERENCES

### *Books and Articles*

Cowan, I., *Jews in Remote Corners of the World*, New York: 1971.

Deutscher, I., *The Non-Jewish Jew & Other Essays*, Oxford: 1968.

Ezra, E.D., *Turning Back the Pages: A Chronicle of Calcutta Jewry*, London: 1986.

Gidney, W.T., *History of the London Society for Promoting Christianity amongst the Jews*, London: 1986.

Hopkins, H.E., *Sublime Vagabond*, Worthing: 1984.

Kehimkar, H.S., *The History of the Bene Israel of India* (1897), Tel-Aviv: 1937.

Pozialov, G., 'The flight of Bukharan Jews from Central Asia and their Immigration to Eretz Israel (1930-50)', in *Pe'amim* 60, Summer 1994, pp. 109-34 (Hebrew).

Reissner, H.G., 'Indian-Jewish Statistics 1837-1941', in *Jewish Social Studies*, 1950, pp. 349-65.

Roland, J., *Jews in British India*, Brandeis University Press, Waltham, Mass. 1989.

Sartorius, J.A., *Notices of Madras and Cuddalore in the Last Century* (London: 1858, pp. 162-4) In W.J. Fischel, 'Bombay in Jewish History in the Light of New Documents from the Indian Archives', in *Proceedings, American Academy for Jewish Reserch*, Vol. 38-9, New York: 1972, pp. 11-44.

Segal, J.B., *A History of the Jews of Cochin*, Vallentine Mitchell, 1993.

Strizower, S., *The Children of Israel: The Bene Israel of Bombay*, Oxford: 1971.

Voigt, J.H., 'Die Emigration von Juden aus Mittelenuropa nach Indien während der Verfolgung durch das NS Regime', *Wechselwirkungen, Jahrbuch 1991. Aus Lehre und Forschung der Universität Stuttgart*, pp. 83-95 (German).

Weil, S., 'Contacts between the Bene Israel and the Holy Land (8th century BCE-1948): An Ethno-historical perspective', in Ben-Ami (ed.): *Sephardi and Oriental Jewish Heritage*, Jerusalem: 1982, pp. 165-78.

———, 'Symmetry between Christians & Jews in India: The Cnanite Christians & the Cochin Jews of Kerala', in T. Timberg (ed.), *The Jews of India*, Delhi: 1986, pp. 177-204.

———, 'Bene Israel', in P. Hockings (ed.), *Encyclopaedia of World Cultures*, Boston: Vol. 3, 1992, pp. 27-9.

———, 'Hierarchy, Religion & Gender: Contradictory Systems of Value among Bene Israel Women in India'. In: Julie Leslie (ed.), *Gender, Religion and Social Definition in India*, New Delhi: OUP (forthcoming).

*Journals referred to:*

*Jewish Advocate.*
*Jewish Tribune.*

# PERSONALITIES AND PROBLEMS

# Walter Kaufmann: A Forgotten Genius

*Agata Schindler*

Walter Kaufmann has largely been forgotten, undeservedly though. Who was he? At the beginning of the 1930s, he was thus characterized: 'A musician with an instinct sure to sweep you off.'[1] On his works, we read: 'Walter Kaufmann's *Symphony in Classical Style* has been received in Karlsbad . . . with a standing ovation.'[2] And further: 'Walter Kaufmann is definitely one of the luckiest talents in music of the young German generation of composers which Czechoslovakia has produced.'[3] Why do we today know so little about him? Who was this talent of the 1930s? What happened to his works?

Walter Kaufmann was a composer, conductor, pianist and musicologist who was born in a German-speaking Jewish family in Karlsbad in 1907. He took his first lessons in music from his uncle Moritz Kaufmann.[4] At the conservatory in Prague, he took violin lessons from Willy Schweyda.[5] In Prague, he also attended classes in theory and composing by Fidelio F. Finke.[6] Studying music initially at the State Academy Conservatory in Berlin[7] as a student of Franz Schreker and Curth Sachs,[8] and then at the German University in Prague[9] musicology under Gustav Backing and Paul Nettl,[10] he did so without the permission and support of his parents.[11] But Walter Kaufmann, a musician with body and soul, soon had his way and nothing appeared to stand in the way of his career as a composer and conductor.

Until his exile, he had a wide variety of influence and interests. His circle of friends and acquaintances included significant names. Existing documents testify contacts with Albert Einstein, Franz Werfel, Max Brod, Heinz Politzer, Otto Pick, Willy Haas and Franz Kafka's family[12] (Gerty Herrmann, Franz Kafka's niece, was his first wife).[13] In the field of music, he worked, amongst others, with Edith Kraus who played many of his compositions—even the *Piano Concerto No. 1*[14] which he had composed in India.[15] He was an assistant to the conductor Bruno Walter at the Charlottenburg Opera in Berlin,[16] and Walter recommended Kaufmann for a post as a second conductor, an offer the latter declined. And likewise, he rejected an offer to work in Prague under the conductor Heinrich Swoboda who performed several compositions of Kaufmann.[17] His work with Ralph Benatzky procured him a well-paid job at the UFA in Neubabelsberg, where he composed, orchestrated and conducted.[18] His compositions were played fairly early by the local Karlsbad orchestra;[19] the Czech Philharmony in Prague played his *Symphony in Classical Style* as early as 1931.[20] He worked as conductor and pianist for Prague Radio[21] as well as for the Berlin and Breslau Radios, making music along with Wilhelm Grosz, a composer who too was to emigrate later.[22] Occasionally, he was engaged as a conductor by the Karlsbad and Eger orchestras.[23] In 1932, he was awarded the Dr Johann Kanka Foundation award for his compositions,[24] and in the same year he won the 'Goethe scholarship' of 'Concordia' in Prague for a musicological essay.[25]

Political events of the early 1930s interrupted his very promising musical career. In 1934,[26] when Prague was considered to be *the* place of exile for the early German emigrants, Kaufmann had already left. He is one of the first Jewish artists[27] who left Bohemia; later these artists comprised an entire generation in exile.

Kaufmann decided to emigrate to India where he worked for twelve years as a composer, conductor and organizer of musical events, founding the Bombay Chamber Orchestra, serving as director of All India Radio, Bombay[28] and assisting other emigrants, e.g. Willy Haas.[29] Thereafter, he had a short stint with the BBC in London, several years in Canada (first at the Conservatory in Halifax, then nine years as a conductor of the newly founded Winnipeg Symphony Orchestra and finally[30] as professor of classical musicology at the Indiana University in Bloomington until his death on 9 September 1984.[31] His efforts to return to Prague or settle down in Israel were in vain; his hopes remained unfulfilled dreams.[32] For almost half a century, he led a life continuously searching for a safe harbour and looking for his old friends lost the world over. He always had to establish new contacts and prove himself afresh. Hence, it is all the more surprising that he found the inner peace to create such an extensive *oeuvre*. He wrote in all more than hundred compositions; he is the author of several unique essays on music ethnology, mainly about Indian music.[33] He was a good conductor, an excellent professor and, last but not least, a versatile librettist of his own stage compositions. He wrote at least nine libretti for his compositions.[34]

Kaufmann's stage compositions form about a fifth of his *oeuvre*. Of these, about twenty-one compositions are known to date: three ballets, one operetta and seventeen operas. Of these, six were composed in his native country, probably during the years 1931-4, some of which were also performed there. All these compositions, like most of his works, have not been published. Even the manuscripts of these six works cannot be located at present; we know very little about them.

In an application for financial support in 1932,[35] Kaufmann referred to the completed overture to his opera *Der grosse Dorin*. He wrote the application in March of that year, which implies that he must have been busy with this opera even before that time. The libretto for the three-act comedy was written by P. Eisner.[36] This librettist was most probably Paul Eisner, journalist, writer and editor of the *Prager Presse*.[37] Until now, we have no further information about this composition.

In 1935, when Kaufmann was no longer in Prague, the journal *Der Auftakt* published several news items referring to him. There we read:

Extraordinary talent in musical composition has also been shown by the young Kaufmann. He is mainly interested in the exotic element in music. His musical palette is as colourful as inexhaustible. His rhythm has a multi-faceted originality. His musical expressions are as strong in lyrical sentimentalism as in the bizarre and ironic. His small opera based on Gogol's *Nase* reveals him as a composer capable of creating a strong impact, full of temperament and spontaneity....[38]

Three years later Erich Steinhard characterized Kaufmann thus: 'An excellent musician full of temperament ... who has written already three stage compositions including a small opera based on Gogol's *Nase*....'[39] We also know that Kaufmann was working on another opera, again based on a work by Gogol, viz., the opera *Der Mantel* which remained unfinished.[40] We do not have any further information about these two works. There are references indicating that Max Brod was the librettist for Kaufmann's opera *Die Nase*.[41] However, Kaufmann does not mention this in his autobiography. Max Brod referred to Kaufmann's *Nase* thus: 'small opera based on Gogol's *Nase* which he [i.e. Kaufmann] just completed (text by Otto Pick) is unique in it's boldness and crass effectiveness. The exotic element, which is the hallmark of this composer, this Gauguin amongst the young Prague composers, is reflected even in the small quartets....'[42] In these references, Max Brod brings to our notice Kaufmann's early interest in non-European music even before his emigration, introducing exotic elements somehow in his compositions, which we are not yet able to substantiate, due to still missing notes, material and sources.

From Kaufmann's autobiography we come to know that Max Brod greatly helped and influenced him. It was he who put Kaufmann in touch with the poet Heinz Politzer. Shortly after their first few meetings, Kaufinann wrote four songs for voice and piano based on poems of Politzer.[43] Before long, Politzer suggested that they jointly write an opera. Kaufmann reminisces:

> The opera was to be an 'Esther', and the story of Esther was really full of dramatic incidents.... After a couple of months, the opera was ready, at least in a rudimentary form. We called it 'Hadassah' and played it for Dr Max Brod, who really gave us valuable advice and praised the work. When we later played for him the work again after making the changes that he had suggested, Brod suggested that we show the opera to Franz Werfel living in Prague at that time.... We spent a whole afternoon with Werfel who was really nice and also highly interested. We left him with his words of praise ringing in our ears. The opera would have progressed, if only the subsequent political situation had been less hysterical. But an Esther-theme in a mentally deranged world was hardly a promising proposition. Well, Heinz and I were young and we dropped it for the time being....[44]

In all probability, the whole enterprise was dropped, not only temporarily but permanently. There is no further trace of this opera.

Through Franz Werfel, Kaufmann got acquainted with another literary person—the librettist Otto Pick. The outcome was a humorous chamber opera *Der Hammel bringt es an den Tag*. This is probably the only stage composition of his pre-exile period which Kaufmann, which although not produced on the stage, was at least heard being performed on radio. It was premièred on 18 March 1934 in the German programme of Prague Radio. The Prague Radio Orchestra played it; Walter Taub lent his voice and the conductor was Heinrich Swoboda.[45] In any case, this performance was one of the last of his own works which Kaufmann was able to hear in his homeland. In the context of this opera, we once more get some concrete evidence of the use of non-European motifs in Kaufmann's creations, viz., Arabic elements.[46] The young composer was obviously quite satisfied with his creation, judging from his comments on this performance when he, almost half a century later, stated: 'Success yes; but a future in this world which is day by day becoming insane, no!'[47]

It is unlikely that, apart from moral recognition, the stage compositions mentioned here brought the young composer any financial advantages. At present it is impossible to state whether these works were ever performed after the end of the war.

Quite a different fate awaited his only three-act operetta *Die weisse Göttin* (*The White Goddess*). Reference works list Felix Kilian and Kurth Juhn as the authors of the text, whereas Kaufmann in his autobiography refers to one author only without giving his name. The composer described the story of this composition thus:

I once wrote an operetta with a friend of mine, a good script and my rather popular music, at least in this case. I really did not like the music when we played it before a famous, wealthy man. I expressed myself in this sense, and the wealthy man replied: 'What? You don't have a very good opinion about your own music? I think it is fantastic!' I gently contradicted him and continued to sip my wine which was much better than the operetta termed by my friend *Die weisse Göttin*. The wealthy man requested us to play a single scene which he had particularly been pleased with once again. When we had played the thing once more and had gone through the text again, the gentleman whose name I unfortunately cannot remember said: 'Listen, my friend, would you be ready to sell me all the rights to your operetta?' I first could not comprehend what he really wanted. Only when he repeated his suggestion, did I begin to realise that I could make some money with this operetta, and, of course, I had no objection. We all sat round the table, my librettist, the wealthy gentleman, his secretary and my little self. 'I herewith offer you ten thousand *Kronen* for the performance rights and the usual copyright' I looked at my librettist who was waiting for a similar offer. And that was also made. I, of course, agreed to sell the rights.[48]

Thus, virtually overnight, Kaufmann came to possess a lot of money.

The aforementioned incident happened in 1934 in Prague, in the days when Kaufmann came to know that a good Jewish friend of his had been trampled to death by Nazis in the streets of Berlin;[49] those were also the days when his thesis on the topic 'Die Instrumentation Gustav Mahlers'[50] was accepted by the German University in Prague.[51] When Kaufmann found that his professor was a committed and well-known Nazi, he wrote a letter to him saying that he could not accept his doctorate from the hands of a Nazi. 'I carried this letter to the post office, went to the biggest travel agent and bought myself a ticket to Bombay with the money I had received for the operetta....'[52]

(Kaufmann eventually got a doctorate in 1956.) Music-lovers in Winnipeg learnt of the occasion:

Walter Kaufmann has been awarded the degree of Doctor of Music honoris causa by the Spokane Conservatory of Music, Spokane, Washington. The degree was awarded on the recommendation of Dr Paul Nettl, Darius Milhaud, William Steinberg and Dmitri Mitropulos with respect to Walter Kaufmann's professional record as composer, conductor and scholar, and academic work completed at the University of Prague in both philosophy and music.[53]

In spite of this development, Prague and Bohemia played an important role in the life of Walter Kaufmann. His decision to flee from his homeland put an end to 27 interesting and formative years of his life as an artist.

*The White Goddess* then began to 'live', albeit at a time when Kaufmann could not personally see it being performed. On 29 June 1935, it was premièred at the Karlsbad town theatre.[54] It was repeated on 8 July,[55] and a cross-section for two pianos was played on Prague Radio on 14 September. The interpreters were the pianists Hermann Noe-Nordberg and Fritz Kerten.[56] The 'wealthy man', mentioned earlier, seems to have been behind these performances. In his memoirs written about 15 to 20 years before his autobiography in German, Kaufmann mentions in connection with this operetta a certain 'Mr Braun'.[57] It is not unlikely that this name refers to the German man of letters Felix Braun who lived in Prague writing librettos as a co-author under the pseudonym 'Felix Kilian'.

In connection with its première, the Karlsbad press offers us some details about the operetta *Die weisse Göttin*. About its creation we learn that the work was to be completed in India, i.e. in 1934/35. Although the 'Bibliography of Walter Kaufmann's Works'[58] gives 1933 as the year of its creation, the operetta had at that time apparently not been completed. Also the above-mentioned sale of the rights to the 'wealthy gentleman' possibly took place even before the work had been completed.

Whether it was destiny or a desire to locate the book or rather the contents of the action of the operetta in Asia (India), in Europe (Karlsbad) or in America and how far the composer himself was involved in inventing this fairy tale are still open questions. We know, however, that the locations of the action of this operetta were significant in Kaufmann's life on these three continents. And we also know that to go to America had always been a dream of the young Berlin student.[59]

After the première of the operetta *Die weisse Göttin*, the press again draws our attention to the 'exotic person' Walter Kaufmann. This time not only with regard to the music but also to the choice of themes, as is obvious from the following extract:

Première of the operetta *Die weisse Göttin* in the Karlsbad town theatre.... A thousand year old rules of Timuraja of Kantagra, rooted in deep piousness, and sanctified, all of a sudden disappear at the call of a dream-like appearance in which the young Timuraja beholds a beautiful damsel of white blood, recognising her as the white goddess. The dream becomes a desire when the king yearns for the fair damsel. Besotted by a burning desire, he leaves his land for Europe to search for her who for a short while had turned his dream into reality in India and fled from there. He finds her again in Karlsbad, where she had followed her bridegroom. In Karlsbad, she disengages her relationship with her fiancé: Eros is strong and uproots all barriers. The Indian king and the white damsel are united in marriage, and at the same time, America blends with India in marriage. Walter Kaufmann has found an astonishing but precise position with regard to this operetta libretto. He discarded the traditional form and type of symphony music and created an original, highly melodious music for the *White Goddess*. The melody in the foreground is of a colourful harmony.... The music is entirely of great aesthetic quality. It is very attractive and invigorating, especially at places where it delves into the Indian interval lengths and sounds. Walter Kaufmann has written a large portion of the musical score in Bombay, on the soil of one of the locations of the operetta.... Kurt Hetzky has done an understanding work in preparing the operetta for the première, so that a good portion of the success was due to his production.[60]

Another critic reporting in some detail about the première, referring for the first time to the jazz elements in Kaufmann's music observes:

Kaufmann's music is noteworthy because it proves that even the lighter style can be raised to a high quality, if it is given a respectable, exclusive and impressive form.... The melody which flows so easily out of Kaufmann's pen is exhilarating, even in the sounds of the exotic.... The pairing of the exotic with the strictly synchronised jazz and the ... waltz. In this operetta music, Kaufmann really cocks a snook at symphonic music.... The symphony artist in Kaufmann need not feel ashamed about this type of music, as he composed only the music of an operetta! ... There were a lot of curtains....[61]

And another pointer to some parts of the operetta being written in Bombay is as follows: 'As Karlsbad and Bombay are located far apart and the post always takes a few weeks to reach, Schroll became the intermediary between the composer and the authors....'[62]

After the première, Kaufmann sent this radio message from Bombay to the Karlsbad theatre director Oskar Basch : 'Hearty congratulations and admiration to you and all the aritsts who made my operetta a success. Yours sincerely, Walter Kaufmann.'[63] This is about all that we know of this stage composition.

For the highly acclaimed première, Kaufmann's father, who lived in Karlsbad, might have helped greatly after Walter had left for India and taken leave on the phone.[64] The farewell by telephone, and not in person, is nowadays really difficult to understand. What was the concrete reason for his hasty departure from Prague? Why did Kaufmann leave for India without discussing the matter with his parents?[65] Were there only the external political reasons for his departure?

What does one take along on such a journey, except memories? For Kaufmann, the memories, positive and negative, played an important role throughout his life. In his thoughts, he lived in Karlsbad, Prague and Berlin. After a long time, he made this note on the première of his operetta: 'About two years later, when I was in India, I read in Prague newspapers which my parents used to send me for a while, that our operetta had its première and the thing was successful. However, this was water down the river....'[66] One may well ask: Water down the river? In spite of innumerable difficulties which a European had to face in Bombay, Kaufmann had soon gained a foothold in the alien land, and, as a director of European music of All India Radio in Bombay, he wrote a new opera *Anasuya*[67] on the occasion of the inauguration of this programme.

The reasons for his undertaking journey to India are given by Kaufmann as follows:

My reason for going to India was relatively simple. I could easily get a visa. I had a friend in Bombay, and inspiring lectures at the university had roused my curiosity, indeed my appetite for this different music. When I heard the gramophone records for the first time, I found the music to be so alien and incomprehensible. However, as I knew that this music was created by people with heart and intellect, one could assume that many, in fact, millions would be appreciating, or in fact, loving this music. As this music was very alien to me, I concluded, that the fault was entirely mine, and the right way would be to undertake a study tour to the place of its origin. A ship of Lloyd Triestino, *Conte Verde*, was scheduled to leave Venice in the next four days, and I found out that I might still manage to catch it if I hurried. My friend in Bombay had assured me that he would provide suitable lodging for me in the first few days. My most difficult task was to explain my plan to my father. Father was in Karlsbad and as it was impossible for me to travel quickly to Karlsbad before my departure for Venice, I had to settle matters over the phone. With a heavy heart, I went to the main post office and called up my father. At first, he was very hesitant, but slowly did we reach an agreement that I would soon get in touch with him from India and that I hoped that the political situation in Europe would improve and that I might perhaps think later of a professional future in my home country. My father, still very angry with me, calmed down slowly and added that a whole lot of the noise around was not based on facts and that lies and meanness would not be able to conquer truth and goodness in the world, that many famous artists were leaving the country to be on the safer side but that they surely would return within a span of weeks or months. And thus, he thought, would also be the case with me. It was quite impossible that so many respected people would find that their world had been snatched away from them, that may last a few weeks but it couldn't last long. I agreed, rather reluctantly, with the opinion of my straight forward and truly innocent father, and we ended our conversation with the assurance that I would concentrate on my doctoral thesis and start my career in real earnest when I once were back from India. In order to take my farewell in a calm mood, I agreed with all the good old man advised, and admitted that the whole political mess would, after all, not end so frightfully as some (in fact, terribly many) had come to believe.[68]

A few days later, probably in spring 1934, Kaufmann left Prague. Although he arrived in India with a return ticket, he never used it for a return journey to Prague. First, he found out that the study of Indian music would take much longer than he had expected. Secondly, he sold off the ticket as he needed the money.[69] Later on, a return journey was just unthinkable. His decision to stay on in Bombay most probably saved his life and that of his wife, who arrived in Bombay on 24 February 1934[70] and was going to teach French at a school.[71]

Immediately on his arrival in Bombay, the family back home received several enthusiastic letters. The journal *Der Auftakt* published short extracts from these letters compiled by Walter's uncle, Moritz Kaufmann. The following extract is taken from this edition, which reveals a lot about Kaufmann's ability to adapt to an alien environment:

I have now been almost a year in India—happy and contented. I am involved here in many things. In Radio Bombay, I head the European department. Apart from my regular concerts, only Indian music, to which I have now formed a strong bond, is transmitted.... My second source of income is my involvement with a large Indo-English film company. I have written a couple of scores for commercial films. I use a lot of Indian motifs. I sometimes write my score for European instruments, but I largely prefer Indian instruments—*sitar, tabla, sagari* and *vina*. I am now familiar even with the Indian and the Urdu notation. I enjoy writing the score in the Indian notation system and presenting it to my musicians. For doing the score for the films, I make extensive use of my collection of Nepalese folk songs and folk dances which I collected shortly after my arrival in Bombay. I have also collected many prayers (prayers to Lord Shiva and Goddess Kali) which have been sung; I also have a large collection of art music. I think, that at present there is no collection of music which is so large and with exact notation as Europeans are prohibited from entering Nepal, i.e. one can go to Nepal if one is lucky to have crossed the thousand hurdles for doing so, which are needed for the permission by the Maharaja. I plan to use this collection for a work on the music of the southern Himalayas. Nepalese music is a strange combination of Indian, Tibetan and Kashmiri music, whereby Kashmiri music also has a lot of Afghani music which is of Persian origin. Apart from this Nepalese collection, I have also done the notation for a collection of pure Indian melodies. It is strange how one gets so involved in a music language so alien to the European and how fast one learns to speak this language. I do not wish to say that my relationship to Western music could somehow be affected on account of my listening and writing a lot of Indian music. Rather, to the contrary. We have regular concerts where, under my direction, we play a lot of good 'Western music'. Our audience which can easily be introduced into Western music comprises mainly Britishers, people from the continent [of Europe], Parsis and Hindus. To this group I recently played, with much success, my piano concert and two new string quartets. Songs to texts of Heinz Politzer have also been written and sung. My third area of activity is chamber music. I have succeeded in forming a chamber music association. In this 'Bombay Chamber Music', I have already given about fifty concerts. My colleagues of the string quartett are Indians. The chamber music association definitely wishes to have first class musicians. Hence, on my recommendation, they have engaged two musicians from Prague for our music concerts. India is unbelievably rich in music. One could fill a thousand volumes and still find oneself at the beginning....[72]

These lines sent first to Karlsbad and then to Prague, where his parents lived since 1938, were definitely not the only ones he sent to his family. Even his friends will surely have received mail from him and this could give us further valuable and concrete insights in to his life in Bombay. The lines quoted offer us very important information about the activities of Kaufmann during his 12 years stay in India.

All of Walter Kaufmann's published scientific works are available to us. It is amazing to note the amount of research he has done as a music ethnologist in the field of Indian music and the way in which he has systematized and historically arranged it. This accomplishment is in addition to his activities as composer, conductor and finally, since 1957, as a professor for classical music theory at the Bloomington

University. In 1936 he had already prepared 'a large collection of Nepalese folk melodies'.[73] In the same year, he spent the summer with his wife in the region of Gauri Shankar.[74] Such and similar 'study tours' were to culminate later in extensive treatises on music ethnology, which he not only researched and prepared but also wrote out himself. On a work planned he commented: 'Besides, I am typing a few musical expressions of Asia, Africa (as far as possible) and Oceania for my dictionary or note-book. So far, I have typed 1114 pages and I assume that the whole thing will amount to about 1600 to 1700 typed pages. For me, it is really a hobby which I started about 50 years back....'[75] In 1981, the festschrift *Music East and West: Essays in Honour of Walter Kaufmann*[76] was published. In the Preface it is stated that Kaufmann's scientific works 'have been recognised throughout the world'. No greater tribute can be paid to the work of a scientific mind!

The result of his research crystallized into seven extensively researched books published during his lifetime. Two of these are standard reference books on Indian music: *The Ragas of North India* (1968) and *The Ragas of South India* (1976). Kaufmann also wrote many articles which made him a specialist amongst music ethnologists. His last book, the publication of which he was actively involved in, was published in 1981 by Deutscher Verlag für Musik in Leipzig. Its title is *Altindien* (Ancient India) published in the series *Musikgeschichte in Bildern* (Music History in Pictures) edited by Werner Bachmann. Bachmann provided me with the extensive correspondence between him and Kaufmann in connection with the publication of this book (1979-84). Kaufmann and Bachmann became friends while preparing the book. They discussed personal matters too. It is astonishing to discover the scrupulous attention to details and the amount of care taken in handling each problem—corrections, proof-reading and additions were jointly done across continents. Shortly before the book appeared, his doctor sent Walter Kaufmann on a holiday. It was perhaps the first time that Walter Kaufmann asked 'for some patience.... My doctor almost fell off his chair when I replied to his question that I had not taken a holiday in the last 24 years ... the University never thought of granting me a sabbatical'.[77] With joy and satisfaction he wrote on 10 April 1982: 'I have received three copies of the book and we have shown the marvellous book to some friends who were equally excited about it.... Will the other copies be sent by ship? As I have already been asked by friends and colleagues whether the book would some day appear in English, I would like to know whether any such plan is being considered for the future.' This, however, was not to happen. But with the publication of the volume *Altindien*, Kaufmann held his seventh book in his hand. His seventh book overall, but his first in German. With this book, his life also slowly completed a full circle. He wrote a book about the music of a country which offered him exile and protection from the 12 years of National Socialism in Europe. The book has been published in the country which caused him to flee from his homeland 50 years before. But finally, after almost half a century, he could enjoy his work again in his mother tongue, which was German.

Unlike the scientific works of Kaufmann, many of his achievements in other fields related to his years in India (and not only those!) have fallen into oblivion. When Kaufmann arrived in India, he found that there was neither a theatre nor an opera house in the European sense of the term. The term 'opera-house' was used for a cinema hall. And the cinema was not very sophisticated. Fairly soon, Kaufmann got acquainted with the Indian film producer Mohan Bhavnani, about whom he wrote: 'He was not particularly successful with the Indian public because he had too much taste. But he was excellent....'[78] Kaufmann composed, *inter alia* the music for Bhavnani's film *The Mill* which was banned as Communist propaganda.[79] From the Bibliography, we know that, in India, he produced numerous scores for 'Information of India' (1935-40)[80] and scores for commercial films (1935-40). About the origin of the films, he wrote in 1945: 'I was in Tibet twice. I have done a 16 mm colour film of Mt. Everest ... I experienced everything possible (I should rather say "impossible"....[81] In the field of films, Kaufmann also cooperated with Willy Haas in Bombay. It was most probably for the film called by Willy Haas *Dorflegendchen* (small legends of the village). Willy Haas wrote the script and Kaufmann composed the music.[82] It is also possible that this refers to the film entitled *Indische Legende* (Indian legend) 'the script of which Willy Haas wrote after long studies of Indian village life and of Indian mythology'.[83]

Very few facts about his work as director of European music of All India Radio in Bombay are known to us. But from a summary of his letters we may conclude that he was the head of the music department as early as 1935. On this work he wrote in a letter to Edith Kraus in 1945: 'You want to know what I am doing. Well, it is fairly simple and not so interesting. I am the key-person in music of All India Radio; I am something like an extraordinary bureaucrat, I do not have a high but "comfortable" income, lots and lots of work, a lot more of intrigues and squabbles and few chances for a "better future"....'[84] The Czech composer Karel Reiner, one of the few in his home country who remembers Kaufmann, wrote of him in 1971: 'It appears that today nobody knows anymore of the gifted composer and conductor Walter Kaufmann of Karlsbad who went to India in the thirties and became the head of the music department in Bombay. I know that we were happy to realise that he continuously propagated our music.'[85] From this information, we may assume that Kaufmann produced the music of his country live on radio for transmission. If the conjectures can be proved, that Bombay Radio still plays the same signature tune which Kaufmann had composed at the time of its inauguration, this would be one of the marks he would have left behind to this day in Bombay. The radio archives of Bombay may be able to deliver some more information on this—as well as on the opera *Anasuya* mentioned earlier.

The present Bombay Chamber Music Society reminds us of its counterpart founded by Kaufmann in 1934. He wrote about the formation of this society as follows:

After I had been in Bombay for about two months, I formed a string quartett—I played the viola—and a trio in which I played the piano. Both Fred [i.e. a friend of Walter Kaufmann] and his brother, who had a lively interest in music, advised and helped me in founding the Chamber Music Society, for which the quartett or the trio would give weekly concerts. They organised a meeting of potential members who all agreed that such a society would be a very good idea and they would like to be members but only under one condition: as they had become a little sceptical about music performances in the city, they insisted on a 'test'. I was quite shocked to hear of this proposal and also a little hurt, but as my friends were greatly interested in founding this society and I badly needed the money, I agreed. The test concert was organised—on this occassion, the trio 'Dumky' by Dvorák was played for the first time in India—and the society was formed. Initially, the concerts were organised at the residences of the members who had large rooms and a piano. Pianos in Bombay are something a newcomer has really got to get used to—they are worse in adjusting to the weather than humans. I can still remember a rather embarassing incident which took place during one of the first concerts of the society. The concert was to take place at the residence of a lady who assured me that her piano was one of the best. I took her word and did not try the piano out. I sat at it in the evening, in a rather good mood, to play Bach's *Chromatic Phantasy and Fugue.* I was most horrified to find out that some keys were jammed, others did not strike at all and the piano was badly tuned. After a brave fight through the first few measures, I stood up and excused myself—it was impossible to continue.[86]

Ernest N. Schaffer also reminisces about the music association:

The 'Bombay Chamber Music Society' was destined to have a major success. The untiring source of inspiration behind it was Walter Kaufmann, an émigré from Prague.... He could already look back upon a great career as a musician.... It was soon a must to attend these weekly concerts. I have in front of me the programme of the 61st chamber concert on 29 August 1935. It lists compositions of Bach, Vivaldi and Kaufmann. The small orchestra comprised emigrants, both male and female, and also the father of Zubin Mehta....[87]

Many new compositions of Kaufmann were created due to his connection with the Chamber Music Society. *Ten String Quartets* (1935-46) and *Three Piano Trios* (1942-6) were probably played first in Bombay. Even the *Indian Piano Concerto* mentioned in his letters seems to have been first performed in Bombay (although hard to imagine) at this association, with Kaufmann at the piano. On 17 January 1937, the piano concerto (which Kaufmann himself referred to as the *Indian Concerto*) was played on Prague Radio. The pianist was Edith Kraus, the conductor Heinrich Swoboda.[88] This piano concert received an overwhelming response in the press at the time:

Walter Kaufmann combines Indian motifs with European forms to create an unimaginably interesting new structure. The set with the dance motif is particularly effective, and the other one with a cantilena shepherd song. The piano as a solo instrument joins in, now leading, now integrated into the interval steps, so alien to our ears.... As a pianist, Ms. Edith Steiner-Kraus has done full justice to the high demands placed on her as a soloist, both from a technical as well as a musical point of view.... One cannot but state that it is a unique, valuable, highly interesting composition by Walter Kaufmann.[89]

One of the leading German newspapers in Prague wrote about this piano performance on the radio:

This noteworthy piece has been written in Bombay.... It is understandable that India exercised a strong influence on his creativity.... The Indian five-tone system, the exotic of a foreign country, the foreign rhythms ... all that has combined to form this Piano Concerto. Even the first movements leading to an Indian dance, the moaning melody of the oboe, and the piano part prepare the mood retained right up to the end. Edith Kraus-Steiner was an excellent interpreter of the difficult but gratifying piece....[90]

This composition has also sunk into oblivion, despite the fact that the full score was in the possession of the composer till 1976. On

25 May 1976, Kaufmann wrote to Edith Kraus from Bloomington:

It was very pleasing, really wonderful, to have you here—even though the visit was quite short. I have searched for the *Indian Piano Concerto* and found it early today. Dear Edith, the concert was written for you. You (along with Heini Swoboda) breathed life into it in Prague and it should remain so. I have never offered the concert to anyone else. It shall remain in your hands! It need not be played again, but you know the piece and it was written only for you, in fact, dedicated to you....

The copy of the full score which I received from Edith Kraus has now been lodged with SOCAN, the representative for author rights of Kaufmann. There may be a publisher who will publish it so that it can be played again. Pianists are definitely interested in this composition.

The other works composed in Bombay include *Six Indian Miniatures* (1943) premièred by BBC in London in 1944 and published by Arcadia in London in 1948. Also, the suite for piano and chamber orchestra *Navaratnam* (1945) was premièred by BBC in London in the year of its creation. The first and second violin concertos were also composed in India (1943 and 1944), of which the last one was premièred in Bombay. Moreover, his work *Picturebook for Katherine* written at the time of the birth of his daughter Katherine in 1944, forms part of his *oeuvre* created in India. Reference works give different dates of its origin; but it is most likely that it was composed in Bombay in 1945.

Although I could not determine the exact year of the composition of Kaufmann's *Nocturne for Orchestra*, it is certain that its première took place on 17 December 1953. The programme leaflet reads: 'This composition represents nocturnal Bombay, perhaps somewhere at the outskirts of the city. It is a quiet place, in which the Oriental night is interrupted by quick dance passages. This *Nocturne* is arranged in the form of a theme and variations, the whole work being based on six notes.'[91] Like many other of Kaufmann's compositions, this work has not yet been published. Although we have some clues from Walter Kaufmann's sojourns in Berlin and Prague, which point to an early use of non-European motifs in his compositions, the years in India, as he himself stated, really 'Indianized'[92] his musical language and his style. This aspect ought to be verified in India.

Kaufmann's years of exile were not always smooth and easy-going. As a refugee, he searched constantly for an inner harmony. In India, where he had also been very ill (tropical flu, malaria, dysentery, etc.),[93] he understandably longed for his native country. Of the stations in his life mentioned, he finally settled down in the USA where he spent the last quarter century of his life. But his years in India shaped him for the rest of his life. In 1984, old and sick and five months before his death, he wrote: 'At present, I am playing a little bit with the folk music of Hindukush, Karakorum, Tibet, Sikkim, etc. I had collected these simple melodies in the thirties and I have just now found the time to organise them. Will I be able to accomplish it? Well, let us see....'[94] However, he did not live to see the publication of his 'Note-book' of non-European music terms referred to earlier. He died on 8 September 1984 in Bloomington.

During his last years, he could still modestly enjoy the fruits of his research in Indian music. In 1945 he had obsevered. 'In the last 10 years, I have rigorously studied the serious art music of India and written a fat book about it. I am sure, nobody will want to read it....'[95] Earlier, he had not thought of a career as a leading specialist in the field of Indian music. The rich Indian source turned the Karlsbad-born Walter Kaufmann into a force to reckon with in musicology. We are still asked to revive his music too.

When Hans Busch, who had left Dresden in 1933 with his father, the conductor Fritz Busch, after the latter was banished from the *Sächsische Staatsoper*, visited Dresden for the last time in April 1996, I had the opportunity of learning a lot about his 15-year friendship with Walter Kaufmann. Hans Busch summarized his opinion about his 'Buddhist brother', as he called him, thus: 'Walter Kaufmann was one of the best and most warm-hearted persons I have ever known. His life was highly influenced by Buddhism. The metaphysical idea was woven into his entire life. He was an excellent musician, a fabulous librettist [Hans Busch staged his productions in the USA], a gifted teacher, a man highly creative, radiant, full of knowledge and humour.'

## POSTSCRIPT

In 1997, while at the Sudetendeutsches Musikinstitut in Regensburg I did some research on ostracized or exiled composers. On that occasion, I came across material about Walter Kaufmann. The sketchy, but extremely valuable information about him made me curious to find out more about him. Based on as much material I had access to, I researched his artistic work and life till the time of his exile. My research led me to correspondence and personal visits to many archives, institutions and contemporaries in the Czech Republic, Germany, the USA, Canada, Israel and India. The early results of this enterprise have been published in the journal *Hudebni veda* of the Czech Academy of Sciences, Prague 1996, Vol. 3, pp. 233-44. I refer here to the extensive source material and references listed there, which have also been the basis of this paper.

This contribution is a revised and extended version of my papers presented at a conference at the Sudetendeutsches Musikinstitut in Regensburg on 17/18 May 1996 and at a seminar organized by the Sangeet Research Academy from 29 November to 1 December 1996 in Bombay.

For assisting me generously with source material I am especially grateful to Professor Edith Kraus, Jerusalem; Professor Hans Busch, Bloomington (who died on 17 September 1996); Dr Herta Haas, Hamburg; and Dr Werner Bachmann, Borna. I would also like to thank the Goethe Institute and Dr Anna Winterberg of the Max Mueller Bhavan in Bombay and Dr Georg Lechner of the Max Mueller Bhavan in New Delhi for supporting me with ideas and material.

## NOTES AND REFERENCES

1. Max Brod, 'Junge Deutsch-Prager in der Musik', in *Der Auftakt, Musikblaetter*, XIII Year, Prague: 1933, Vol. 3/4, pp. 39-40.
2. *Der Auftakt*, X Year, Prague: 1930, Vol. 12, p. 298.
3. *Der Auftakt*, XIII Year, Prague: 1933, Vol. 5/6, p. 82.
4. Moritz Kaufmann, born in 1871, graduate of the Prague Conservatory, owner of the music school in Karlsbad, music expert and critic, composer, in *Deutsche Tonkuenstler und Musiker in Wort und Bild*, Friedrich Jansa (ed.), Leipzig: Friedrich Jansa Publishers, 1911, pp. 337f. Moritz Kaufmann died in 1943 in a concentration camp; see Rudolf M. Wlaschek: *Biographiae Judaica Bohemiae*, Johannes Hoffmann (ed.), Veroeffentlichungen der Forschungsstelle Ostmitteleuropa an der Universitaet Dortmund, Series B, Vol. 52, Dortmund, 1995, p. 102. The stations of deportation of Moritz Kaufmann have been documented in the publications of Theresienstadt Initiative (Terezinská pametní kniha, Prague: Melantrich 1995) thus: Moritz Kaufmann was deported by the transport Aaq on 13 July 1942, from Prague to Theresienstadt and by the transport Bw on 19 October 1942, from Theresienstadt to Treblinka.
5. Paul Nettl, 'Kaufmann, Walter', in *Die Musik in Geschichte und Gegenwart* (abbrev. MGG), Vol. 7. Kassel: Bärenreiter, 1958, p. 760.
6. While talking about his students, Fidelio F. Finke put Walter Kaufmann

at the top of the list. The discussion took place in 1966 in connection with the preparation of Dieter Haertwig's thesis for 'habilitation' on Fidelio F. Finke.

7. In the file 'Angelegenheiten der Schueler' (Student Matters), there is an entry dated 6 October 1926, where Walter Kaufmann's studentship is confirmed in connection with some passport matters. In the annual reports, Kaufmann has been confirmed to be a student from October 1926 to October 1927. Hochschule der Kuenste (College of Arts), Hochschularchiv, Berlin, Bestand 1, Nr. 559.
8. Walter Kaufmann describes his relationship with Franz Schrecker and Curth Sachs as follows: 'Franz Schrecker was a wonderful teacher and I valued him a lot. But my highest regard is reserved for my other teacher at the music college, Dr Curt Sachs. He was an unbelievably learned teacher who taught me to first organise my thoughts before I wrote down anything and to continue and extend my studies of musical instruments not only of the West but also of the Far East. He was a good, wise teacher and friend whom I owe a lot . . .,' in Walter Kaufmann, 'Autobiography' (in German language), Ms., no date and title page, typed, corrected and paginated manually, 83 pages, p. 22. The autobiography comprises the memoirs of Walter Kaufmann till 1934 and was written in the 1970s in Bloomington. Hans Busch states that he had suggested it (conversation of the author with Hans Busch on 18 April 1996 in Dresden). Copy in the collection of the author.
9. Walter Kaufmann studied at the University of Prague from winter semester 1927/28 till the summer semester 1931. Information by the Institut für Geschichte, Karls University in Prague, 12 July 1996 (original in Czech language).
10. Refer to note 5.
11. Refer to note 8, p. 10.
12. Walter Kaufmann's handwritten application to the 'Deutsche Gesellschaft für Wissenschaften und Künste in der Cechoslovakischen Republik' for granting financial support. Prague, 4 March 1932. Copy of material from the Central Archive of the Czechoslovakian Academy of Sciences; Archive, Sudetendeutsches Music Institute, Regensburg.
13. Refer to note 8, p. 57. Walter Kaufmann already in India and Gerty Herrmann still in Prague married by proxy (information by the pianist Edith Kraus in an interview with the author in February 1996 in Jerusalem). In 1944, their daughter Katharine was born, now living in the United States. From Walter Kaufmann's application to the 'Deutsche Gesellschaft für Wissenschaften und Künste' (see note 12) we learn that, in 1932, he was living in Prague, at first at 6/III Altstädter Ring, and later at No 4, Bílkova Str., Mrs Kafka's flat. As both these addresses are connected with flats of the Kafka family, it is most likely that it was there that he also came to know Gerty, Franz Kafka's niece.

Hans-Gerd Koch of the Bergische Universität-Gesamthochschule Wuppertal, editor of the critical edition of Kafka's works, provided the author with this information: 'In 1931, Walter Kaufmann was in contact with the Herrmann family, and was a friend of Felix (i.e. his later brother-in-law) with whom he made a holiday trip, visiting amongst other places the Grossglockner. This may be concluded from a letter of Elli Herrmann to her sister Valli.' Information by letter of 14 March 1996. Collection of the author.

14. The concert took place on 17 January 1937 on Prague Radio. In Eckhard Jirgens, card index of the radio assistants of the German transmission in the first CSR (Program bulletin, *Deutscher Rundfunk der Tschechoslowakei,* March 1927-May 1939), Schwelm 1994 ff.
15. 'Der Querschnitt' (excerpts from the letters of Walter Kaufmann—the author). In: *Der Auftakt*, XV Year, Prague 1935, p.142.
16. Refer to note 8, pp. 43-6.
17. In Radio Prague, the following compositions of Kaufmann were played under the baton of Heinrich Swoboda: the opera *Der Hammel bringt es an den Tag* on 18 March 1934 (première), *Symphony for Strings* on 21 April 1935, *First Piano Concerto* (also referred to as the *Indian Piano Concerto*) on 17 January 1937 (played for the first time after its première in India) as well as the *Third Symphony* on 17 May 1937. From Extracts from the *Radio Journal,* 1932-8, prepared by the Central Archives of Czechian Radio in Prerov and Labem, 1995. (Original in Czech language in the collection of the author.) Walter Kaufmann's reference to his cooperation with Heinrich Swoboda in his autobiography, p. 54; refer to note 8.
18. Refer to note 8, pp. 40 and 44.
19. The première of his *Suite im alten Stil fuer Streicher* was on 31 March 1929. Source: Program sheet, original, collection of the author.
20. Program sheet of the extraordinary concert of the Czech Philharmony on 8 February 1931. Original in the archive of the Czech Philharmony in Prague.
21. Concerts on 14 June 1932, 6 November 1932, 26 March 1933, and 12 November 1933, in Extracts from the *Radio Journal*, 1932-8; refer to note 17.
22. Concert on 4 February 1939 (position no. 3557) and on 18 November 1932 (position no. 3469) in the Breslau radio station, and on 7 December 1930 (position no. 3469) in Berlin, in Catalogue of the Reichsrundfunkgesellschaft in the Deutsches Rundfunkarchiv (German Radio Archives), Frankfurt am Main.
23. Walter Kaufmann, article in *The New GROVE Dictionary of Music and Musicians*, Vol. 9, London: 1983, p. 833.
24. Letter by the German Society of Sciences and Arts of the Czechoslovakian Republic to Walter Kaufmann, 9 December 1932. Material

of Ustrední archiv Ceskoslovenské akademie ved (Central Archive of the Czechoslovakian Academy of Sciences), document no. 592/1932. Copy of this document in the Sudetendeutsches Musikinstitut, Regensburg.

25. *Der Auftakt*, XII Year, Prague 1932, p. 116.
26. In the introduction to 'Der Querschnitt' (from the letters of Walter Kaufmann), it is stated: 'The composer Walter Kaufmann has left his domicile [i.e. Prague] a year ago....' in *Der Auftakt*, XV Year (refer to note 15).
27. As proof of his Jewish origin, there is a copy of his entry in the Jewish community in Karlsbad (letter dated 25 August 1995 from the Czechian Embassy to the author). According to Edith Kraus (information by telephone to the author on 9 January 1996), Walter Kaufmann's mother was of Christian faith: The author has come across a document from the file about the religious faith of the Kaufmann family, dated 15 November 1946, in which Walter Kaufmann's mother explains: '... 30 years ago I married Julius Kaufmann who was of Jewish origin. Hence, I had to flee with my husband in the autumn 1938 from the border area for fear of Nazi occupation to Prague where my husband died. I should also mention that I got converted to the Jewish faith, and hence the Nazis were on my trail in various ways.' The original of this document in Czech language is located in Státni okresni archiv Karlovy Vary (State archive of Karlsbad), Mest NV Karlovy Vary II.
28. Refer to note 15.
29. Voigt, Johannes, H., 'Die Emigration von Juden aus Mitteleuropa nach Indien waehrend der Verfolgung durch das NS-Regime' (the emigration of Jews from Central Europe during the Persecution by the NS-Regime), in *Wechselwirkungen. Jahrbuch 1991. Aus Lehre und Forschung der Universität Stuttgart*, p. 84.
30. Refer to note 5.
31. Mentioned in a letter from David Lasocki, School of Music, Indiana University, 9 August 1995, Bloomington (collection of the author).
32. Walter Kaufmann's letters to Edith Kraus, 26 June 1946 from Bombay; 9 March 1951 and 21 October 1955 from Winnipeg. Private collection.
33. Bibliography of Walter Kaufmann's Works, in Thomas Noblitt (ed.), *Music East and West: Essays in Honour of Walter Kaufmann,* New York: Pendragon Press, 1981, pp 381-6. Heinrich Simbriger, *Werkkatalog zeitgenössischer Komponisten aus den deutschen Ostgebieten.* Supplementary Volume 5, edited by Die Künstlergilde e. V, Esslingen/Neckar, no date, preface (of 1974).
34. Thomas Noblitt, op. cit., p. 383. Refer to note 33.
35. Walter Kaufmann's handwritten application to the 'Deutsche Gesellschaft für Wissenschaften und Künste in der Cechoslovakischen Republik'. Refer to note 12.

36. Orchestral concert of the Prague German programme. Refer to note 14.
37. Refer to note 4 (p. 42).
38. Edwin Janetschek, 'Die jüngsten sudetendeutschen Tonsetzer', in *Der Auftakt*, XV Year, Prague 1935, Vols. 7-8, p. 127.
39. Vladimír Helfert and Erich Steinhard, *Die Musik in Der Tschechoslowakischen Republik*, 2nd (partially revd) edn. Prague: Orbis Verlag, 1938, p. 188.
40. Jitka Ludvová, Ceskoslovenské státní ceny pro nemecké hudebníky (Czech State Awards for German Musicians), in *Hudební veda, Rocník XXXII, Ustav pro hudební vedu AV CR.*, Prague 2/1995, p. 105.
41. Vera Vyslouzilová, 'Max Brod as Translator and Librettist', in *Der jüdische Beitrag zur Musikgeschichte Boehmens und Maehrens*, Regensburg: Sudetendeutsches Musikinstitut, 1994, p. 36.
42. Refer to note 1.
43. Refer to note 5.
44. Refer to note 8, p. 56.
45. Refer to note 15.
46. Orchestra Concert of the Prague German Radio Programme. Refer to note 14.
47. Refer to note 8, p. 56.
48. Ibid., pp. 71f.
49. Ibid., pp. 58-61.
50. Orchestral Concert of the Prague German Radio Programme. Refer to note 14.
51. Walter Kaufmann to Heinrich Simbriger, Bloomington 5 May 1974. Original is with Die Künstlergilde, Regensburg. The letter from the Insitut für Geschichte of the Karls University in Prague of 12 July 1996 to the author informs that the protocol of the viva of the Philosophical Faculty of the German University does not mention the name of Walter Kaufmann. The thesis was not submitted and hence not kept (in Czech language).
52. Refer to note 8, pp. 72ff.
53. In Winnipeg Symphony Orchestra, programme handout, 12 January 1956. Archive of the Winnipeg Symphony Orchestra.
54. In *Karlsbader Tagblatt*, 29 June 1935—announcement of the première under 'Mitteilungen der Theaterkanzlei'.
55. In *Karlsbader Tagblatt*, 5 July 1935, p. 3.
56. Extract from the *Radio Journal*, 1932-8. Refer to note 17.
57. Indian Rhapsody, unfinished and unorganized manuscript of Walter Kaufmann's memoirs written in English. Collection of the author.
58. Thomas Noblitt (ed.), op. cit., p. 383. Refer to note 33.
59. After nearly 50 years, Walter Kaufmann had the following story to tell: 'I intentionally do not want to write here about the incomprehensible

and inhuman mental illness of a people in Central Europe, the early animal symptoms of which could already be noticed during my summer stay in Karlsbad. One afternoon I visited a friend of my father, Mr Gustav Kraus [the father of the pianist Edith Kraus] ... and Mr Kraus invited me to his house for dinner because Mr Friml, a famous Czech composer, now living in Hollywood, had also been invited and on this occasion I might play him a few of my compositions. So I arrived at the Kraus Villa in the evening and all was fine. But I was a dumb idiot: of course, I had the vague hope of once going to America ... my real talent was writing beautiful and useful film music.... I did not know that Friml was on the lookout for such a melody maker. In my stupid vanity, I played him my last *Suite for Orchestra*, very modern, with all possible dissonances ... which did not even get an applause from some musicians in Berlin. So I jangled and tinkled on the piano until I noticed that Friml was absolutely bored.... And, as I came to realise during the next few days, the music I had played to Friml was the most stupid I could ever have presented. Edith told me a few days later that Friml believed that I was talented but felt that with my music, I was on a totally wrong track.In Walter Kaufmann, Autobiography, p. 26. Refer to note 8.

60. In *Deutsche Tageszeitung (Karlsbader Badeblatt)*, 2 July 1935, p. 4.
61. In *Karlsbader Tagblatt*, 3 July 1935, p. 4.
62. Ibid.
63. In *Karlsbader Tagblatt*, 11 July 1935, p. 5.
64. Refer to note 8, pp. 74ff.
65. Ibid.
66. Refer to note 57.
67. Ibid.
68. Refer to note 8, pp. 74ff.
69. Refer to note 57.
70. Ibid.
71. From a letter by Marianne Steiner, cousin of Franz Kafka, to the author. London, 4 April 1996.
72. Refer to note 15.
73. Orchestral concert of the Prague German Radio Programme. Refer to note 14.
74. Ibid.
75. From Walter Kaufmann's letter to Werner Bachmann, Bloomington, 7 October 1982.
76. Refer to note 33. Preface.
77. From Walter Kaufmann's letter to Werner Bachmann, 12 January 1981.
78. Refer to note 57.
79. Ibid.
80. Refer to note 33, p. 384.

81. Walter Kaufmann's letter to Edith Kraus, Bombay, 13 September 1945. Private Collection.
82. Oral information by Dr Herta Haas, widow of Willy Haas, to the author.
83. Refer to note 29, p. 86.
84. Walter Kaufmann's letter to Edith Kraus. Refer to note 81.
85. Karel Reiner, 'Komentár k zivotopisu' (Remark about the bio-data), 1971, manuscript, typed. Refer to p. 110, original in Czech language. Private collection.
86. Refer to note 57.
87. Ernest N. Shaffer, *Ein Emigrant entdeckt Indien*, München: 1971, p. 20.
88. Refer to note 21.
89. In *Karlsbader Abendblatt*, 21 January 1937.
90. In *Prager Tagblatt*, 19 January 1937.
91. In Programme handout of the Winnipeg Symphony Orchestra, 17 December 1953. Archive of the Winnipeg Symphony Orchestra.
92. Walter Kaufmann's letter to Edith Kraus, Bombay, 26 June 1946. Private collection.
93. From Walter Kaufmann's letter to Edith Kraus, Winnipeg, 9 March 1951. Private collection.
94. From Walter Kaufmann's letter to Werner Bachmann, Bloomington, 19 April 1984.
95. From Walter Kaufmann's letter to Edith Kraus, Bombay, 13 September 1945. Private collection.

1. Walter Kaufmann as a student.

2. Walter Kaufmann in later years in America.

Walter Kaufmann,
Rewa House, Warden Road,
Bombay 26.

June 26th,1946.

Meine liebe Edith,

vielen schoenen Dank fuer Deinen lieben Brief und dass Du Dich ein bischen um meine liebe alte Mutter gekuemmert hast. Ich schreibe heute in grosser Eile - also nur ein paar Worte.Da Du nun bei Miss Steiner wohnst,die ich sehr herzlich gruessen lasse,kannst Du sie bitte fragen ob sie weiss wo Dr Heinrich Swoboda zu finden ist,d,h.ob sie seine Adresse weiss,was er tut,etc.

Dann,es sieht so aus als ob meine Berufung an die Prager Universitaet wahr werden wuerde.Bitte gib mir Deine ehrliche offene Meinung ob Du glaubst dass man heutzutage nach Prag gehen soll oder nicht.Gut,ich bin British Subject,aber man hoert so viele ganz widersprechende Ansichten. Manche sagen:um Himmels Willen,gehen Sie nicht nach Prag- andere wieder meinen dass die Lage dort ganz gut sei,etc.Also wie ist es eigentlich wirklich ?

Ich werde Dir,sobald ich kann,etwas von meiner neuen Klaviermusik senden und wenn sie Dir gefaellt und wenn Du Lust hast sie zu spielen wuerde ich mich sehr freuen. Aber ich werde gar nicht gekraenkt sein wenn Du mir sagst dass sie Dir nicht gefaellt.Seit dem Klavierkonzert hat sich mein Stil noch weiter ver-Indert und es ist halt unsicher ob so etwas den Leuten gefallen wird.Nun,wir werden ja sehen. Da ich bis jetzt keine Geld-Ausfuhr nach USA bewilligt kriege,bemuehe ich mich (falls mit Prag nichts wird oder falls das nach Prag Gehen nicht sehr su empfehlen ist) nach England zu kommen.Falls ich dort bei der BBC ( die immerhin viel Interesse an mir haben) eine Stellung bekommen sollte,koennten wir dort meine 3 Klavierkonzerte machen und vieles mehr.

Was sind Deine - oder vielmehr Eure Plaene.Du schreibst gar nicht wie Dein zukuenftiger Mann heisst,was er tut,usw. Bitte gruess ihn recht schoen von mir und ich wuensche Euch alles Glueck fuer die Zukunft. Bitte schreib mir bald und beantworte mir die paar Fragen - ich moechte so gerne wieder mit Swoboda in Kontakt kommen.

Alles Liebe

Dein Walter

3. (Last?) Letter of Walter Kaufmann to Edith Kraus,
Bombay, 26 June 1946.

Für Edith Kraus

I

Andante sostenuto (Pelog:)

(♩ = 80)

Fl. 1 1 2

Harfe

poco rit. ........ a tempo

I. Violinen II.

Bratsche

Cello

Bass

4. Walter Kaufmann's 'Indisches Klavierkonzert'
('Indian Piano Concerto'), first page of score.

# Willy Haas and Exile in India

*Anil Bhatti*

Willy Haas was an *homme de lettres*, i.e. a man of letters, and one of the great literary editors of Germany's legendary second Weimar period. He was also one of the first avant-garde film critics and film script writers, apart from being an essayist, raconteur, friend and critic of writers like Kafka and Werfel. From 1925 to 1932 he edited one of the most widely respected literary journals in Germany and Europe: *Die Literarische Welt.*[1] He was probably one of the greatest classic *feuilletonists* in the German tradition.

Haas was born on 17 June 1891 in Prague, which at that time was in the Austro-Hungarian Empire, and all through his life, which took him from Prague to Berlin, to Bombay, to London and finally to Hamburg, he retained the consciousness of the problems of the legal identity associated with a Central European citizen of the Austro-Hungarian monarchy in its dying phase.

Haas' family was of Spanish-Jewish origin that had migrated to a Moravian village from Holland in 1680. As Haas put it in a charmingly written *curriculum vitae*, he thus 'was born in Prague of a respectable Czechoslovak family that had been settled on Czechoslovakian soil for at least 250 years according to available records'.[2] His father, Dr Gustav Haas, was apparently a well-known and respected lawyer. In the multilingual milieu of Prague, however, to be Jew was almost identical with being German, and both were hated. But, there were exceptions. Haas remembered mobs going on rampages as a child against the German-speaking Jewish community and in one of these attacks their house was saved by their Czech nurse.[3] Like many other intellectuals of his generation, Haas retained a degree of what might be called a clear insight into the inevitability of the collapse of the multilingual, multicultural, transnational Austro-Hungarian empire and the end of the Utopian myth of the Hapsburgs.

Haas was in no sense a nationalist. On the contrary, he was a Weltbürger, a citizen of the world. A state citizenship, documented by a passport, was, however, a critical condition for survival for any emigré. Statelessness was a fear that haunted refugees and exiles.[4] By birth Haas was a citizen of the Austro-Hungarian empire. After the collapse of the Danube monarchy, his native city of Prague became the capital of independent Czechoslovakia and his nationality became Czech. He was, however, a German-speaking Czech, who repeatedly affirmed his love for the German tradition he had inherited. Intellectually, he was at home in Berlin. Fascism, however, forced him to emigrate to India, where he used the Czech version of his name Vilem Haas. In India he became His Majesty's subject and returned to Germany with this legal identity. Only in 1950 did he formally adopt German citizenship.[5]

By 1932 it had become clear to Haas that he would have to leave Germany which was in the grip of Fascist domination. He returned to Prague in 1933, where he worked as editor and script-writer. After Hitler's entry into Prague he decided to leave Europe. Although there was the possibility of getting an American visa, he chose instead to accept the offer of his friend Walter Kaufmann, the composer, who was already in India working with the All India Radio in Bombay.[6] Through the mediation of Paul Claudel, Haas was able to go from Prague to the south of France, where he could meet some of his friends from Prague, among them Franz Werfel. He reached Bombay in June 1939, where a post as a scenario-writer with Bhavnani Productions was waiting for him. A film version of Ibsen's *Ghosts*, *The Legend of the Dead Eyes*, which he called an 'Indian religious village story of my own invention' and a scenario *Kanchan*, in which the actress Leela Chitnis played the leading role, were the creative results that Haas mentions.[7] He also collaborated with Kaufmann on two operas, which were apparently produced by All India Radio. In addition Haas wrote a large number of essays and sketches on a wide range of topics such as the question of Hindu widows or German Jews, which were published in Indian journals. Of special interest are an anthology of German poetry in English translation titled *Germans beyond Germany* (1942), an essay on Kafka and a series of articles 'On Teaching German Literature' published in the *Punjab Educational Journal* (1944/45).[8]

There are many aspects of Haas' life and experiences in India which deserve greater attention. I would like to refer briefly only to his attempts as a litterateur to come to terms with 'India' as presented in his autobiographical recollection and to some comparative cultural reflections in his essays. Like all reconstructions his autobiographical recollection of India is also a construct in which the site of India as a place of exile is justified by an achieved awareness between conscious individual choice and inevitability. An individual acts out a personal history, the prefiguration of which he only becomes aware of in the form of a subsequent epiphanic realization. Given Haas' literary background, it is not surprising that this is articulated through a literary association. In this context Kipling's *Kim* and Gandhi function as *chiffres* for Haas' elective affinity to the country of his exile. Rediscovering *Kim* is one of the central passages of Haas' autobiography. As in all autobiographical reconstruction, Haas too tried to establish a secret pattern of life that unfolds itself gradually through the course of life's journey. Political reasons forced Haas to leave Europe. But why did he choose India? One of the reasons, he subsequently realized while in exile was Kipling's *Kim*, which he had read as a boy. The daughter of one of his Indian friends in Lahore showed him the famous canon, *Kim's* gun, with which the novel's action begins. A strange restlessness gripped Haas and he re-reads this book in one night with amazement, disbelief and indeed horror (LW 260).

It seemed to him that subconsciously he had retraced the path of the narrative action of the book as an exile in India. He actually knew all the places in the book. All the places he had dreamed about when as a young boy he had first read Kipling's novel and he had forgotten that he knew these places. Only now, while reading the book again, he remembered.

Had the complicated preparations of his youth, he queries, been made by Providence for this? Did Professor Moritz Winternitz's lectures on Indology at the University of Prague and the study of Paul Deussen's translations of Indological texts take him towards India. He recalls seeing an Indian film in Venice in 1937 and wondering if he could ever work as a script writer for an Indian film production. (LW 261). And now he was in India. Fate, however, had sent him to India in a somnambulant state, so that he had been unable to recognize the dream world of his childhood. His wish had been fulfilled in an ironic and indeed malicious manner. It had come too late. Now he was over 50 years old.

Life in India had been a stage play with pain, laughter, and joy; but its meaning lay below the surface. *Kim* was the climax leading to an epiphanic awareness:

I had the feeling that after this magical moment I would not experience anything in India. I felt myself to be indescribably near to Fate, to Providence, to a mysterious, clever, unbelievably inventive and infinitely ironic being, which I would not call 'God', although that is exactly what I would like to do. It was like a demiurge of the Gnostics, who had fulfilled everything that fate had decreed, exactly, but completely in reverse. (LW 262)

Almost in keeping with one of the laws of fiction, according to which the final insight into all the ramifications of narrative complexity also closes the narrative, it became clear to Haas that his time in India was coming to an end. Nothing remained after the war was over to really keep him in India. Although, as a British citizen, he could have lived in India, he felt the need to live in a German-speaking environment. His considerations were, however, not tinged with any 'sweet feelings of home'. It was merely the necessity of building up a new existence. As he says: 'I was already over 50—much too late to put down roots anywhere' (LW 262).

Haas left India for Europe in March 1947. The news of Gandhi's assassination (30 January 1948), reached him in London. Gandhi and the principle of non-violence constituted the second reconstructive *chiffre* for his affinity to India. Already as a young man he had affirmed a Tolstoyan fundamental pacifism and probably around the First World War he had read Romain Rolland's book on Gandhi. As he writes: 'I wanted to see Gandhi's country. And I have seen Gandhi's country.' (LW 266). And it is around the shock of the news of Gandhi's assassination that Haas puzzles out his complex relationship to 'Gandhi's country'.

He remembers holy men who wore masks so that they would not inadvertently kill an insect. He remembers a servant who refused to kill a snake and instead carried it carefully away into a nearby jungle. He also saw a dying, suffering cow that nobody would kill. And one of them had gone and killed the one person who preached the sanctity of life.

Clearly, Haas' epiphanic re-discovery of Kipling's *Kim*, and the shock over the assassination of Gandhi cannot but generate the gesture ot the futility of understanding the 'difference'. Haas ultimately decides in his autobiographical reconstruction to leave the plane of intellectual understanding and analysis. The only satisfactory possibility to demonstrate his empathy for India was to leave the terrain of discursive articulation and situate himself in the epiphany of non-verbal recognition:

I have seen it once on an evening in a dirty bazaar street in a village, and I will never forget it. It was in a small brightly lit open shop, in which a woman squatted on the floor with her family. With red colour she drew the holy sign on the foreheads of her husband and her children, decorated them with garlands and handed them food with her small dark hands. And she smiled. She was by no means a beautiful woman, but a Leonardo da Vinci would not be able to paint her smile. I have loved this Indian smile so much, that I have learnt to waken it on the countenance of almost every Hindu child by smiling at it with love and affection. It is a smile full of dreams and sufferings; it is the first weak reflection of a distant and future non-existence, of the sublime merging with the world-soul. It is the unforgettable magic of India, more than the Taj Mahal, more than the cave temples of Ajanta and Elefanta [*sic*], more than the Shalimar Gardens of Shah Jahan.[9]

Such passages may not be very far from kitsch. But they have been contextualized within a comparative cultural meditation and the metaphor of a 'love' which, as it were, transcends difference, and is none the less, based on a conscious awareness and conceptualization of difference. This aspect is articulated in an essay on 'Indische Probleme' published in 1946 in the famous *Die Neue Rundschau*, which at that time was still being brought out from Sweden by the Bermann-Fischer Verlag. Here, Haas would speak with the intellectual authority of the former editor of *Die literarische Welt* and the political anti-Fascist credentials of a European exile, living in India.

India's crisis, Haas claims—and he was referring to the post-war and pre-independence phase—was not just a political one. To understand it, he stressed that Europeans must demarcate some fundamental concepts which differ essentially between India and Europe as far as their thought content and emotional connotations were concerned. Haas referred to the concept of history, historical action and historical development (understood as progress) (NR 81).

Haas approached this problem by first referring to the concept of history as he saw it articulated in the Old Testament. The Jewish philosophy and analysis of history are concerned with the history of their sins and penance, virtues and rewards; in other words with divine vengeance. Jewish historical research, therefore, becomes a search for the sin or virtue responsible for unhappiness or happiness respectively. This, Haas asserted was true for Hinduism and its concept of history also, but with a completely different accent and range. Here it is not just a question of man, but of nature in its entirety, whether animate or inanimate. Above this nature there is not just any God, but a precise mechanism of guilt or crime and punishment that is impersonal. For this mechanism does not exclude anything, be it human, natural or divine.

It is not necessary here to explain how this essential dichotomy between an individual retribution that can be genealogically codified and a non-personal order of things leads to two essentially different societies. One, the European, which is fundamentally mutable and the other, Indian, which is fundamentally immutable. This fundamental immutability also means that tradition cannot be changed in the sense that it is radically eradicated. This interpretation, however, has nothing to do with volition. Haas tried to maintain as neutral a tone as possible in his essentialist diagnosis. The believer in an idol and the believer in an intellectual divine principle are neither better nor worse as Hindus. All that matters is that their place in the cosmic order be fixed.

India then represented to Haas, fundamentally an 'ahistorical idea of history' and its social changes were anti-political politics. India's crisis lies in the fact that two forces, two 'metaphysical' factors were attempting to reconcile these with the real world of historical and political action. One was the *Gita* and the other was Gandhi. But, as Haas pointed out, the philosophy propounded in the *Gita* was the precursor to one of the bloodiest wars depicted and justified in world literature. Hindu-Muslim riots too co-existed with Gandhi in India's world. From Haas' point of view, which in this case follows the tradition of 'Orientalism', this co-existence ('sowohl-als auch' instead of 'entweder-oder') resulted from the metaphysical dissociation of action from volition.

In this context then the role of the Congress Party (and Gandhi, Haas wrote, was still its 'nominal leader') consisted simply in 'introducing Western nationalism and political activism into the Indian social psyche, in covering the many historical and geological layers of India with yet another layer, a layer, which sociologically is identical with the poor and disgracefully underpaid class of the urban Indian intelligentsia' (NR 88).

The attempt by the Congress to forge an essentially cult-oriented and particularistic community into a new nation was comparable to the efforts of the Jewish agency to take the Jews out of their geographic diaspora by creating a modern Israeli state. In both cases an essentially traditional people were being led into the 'promised land'(!) of a modern industrial state (NR 88). Wisely, Haas uses the prerogative of the essayist and refrains from any kind of prognosis.

Examples that Haas chose to depict this co-existence may have derived from his own social experiences:

This modern Indian lady discusses Baudelaire, Rimbaud, T.S. Eliot, Huxley (obviously) and Hemingway with great intelligence. But she still dresses in the way her ancestors have been doing for centuries: in a saree, which however is the most graceful dress ever to adorn a completely feminine body. She is not only *called* Uma or Parvati or Sarasfati [*sic*], but she also looks like a dark mythological goddess. The furnishings in her house however resemble a sale in the department store Wertheim around 1910. No Greek dancer on a marble frieze can imitate a small Indian village girl who runs after her rolling bangles laughing and with hair flying. But her father is decked out in a random mixture of old American, English and Indian clothes like a clown in Circus Barnum. The dead are burnt near the holy Ganges with sandalwood, but the crematoriums are protected against the rain with horrible rusty asbestos sheets; the cremation, which often lasts for hours, reminds one with its atmosphere of complete indifference, of the roasting of a chicken on an open fire. Tradition means simultaneously everything and nothing to the Indian. (NR 87)

It is important to emphasize that in his numerous attempts to come to terms with a theory of India, Haas took great care to differentiate between the popular European prejudices concerning India and a philosophical understanding. Haas, for instance, did not fall prey to the widely prevalent myth of the lazy native, which, colonial writing had popularized. Instead, like many European liberal sympathizers with India he preferred to write: 'It is often said that the Indian is indolent and passive. That is not true. The Indians are one of the most diligent peoples on the face of the earth.' For Haas, the 'problem' lay elsewhere. And by placing it elsewhere he erected an insurmountable structure of *demarcation*. According to Hass: 'Time runs differently in India from what it does in Europe.' Or again: 'The Hindu is not a fatalist.' A remark that would be rare to find in popular literature on India. The Hindu, however, is not a fatalist 'in the sense in which a Mohammedan is one. Kismet and Karma are exact opposites' (LW 292).

One of the interesting points resulting from this observation is the absorption by Haas of a theory of the Indian predilection for the abstract, which precludes modern art. In Haas' view, the whole movement of Western art was towards an aesthetics of relations between the fleeting moment and the permanent, and in capturing the transient you saw the infinite. India's movement was essentially the opposite: 'Indian art achieves its apotheosis not in a portrayal of the eternal through the fleeting moment, of the permanent through the transient, of God through nature, but in the opposite: change through the permanent, the (ever) changing through identity.'[10]

It is possible to interpret this view by suggesting that, according to Haas, the Western tradition sought to discover the symbol, whereas the Indian tradition was essentially allegorical so that what was 'missing in Indian art is the secret meaning beyond that which is portrayed, even when the portrayal in Indian art is of a very high quality' (Merkur 867). This restatement of classic German idealistic aesthetics was, however, not his real point.

The essential difference lay in the fact that time and space were occupied in India by mythology, whereas in Occidental art, these were thrown open to art and, therefore, by implication, to imagination. The argument revolved around secularization. Therefore, modern Indian art was not really possible, because it was either a cheap imitation of the West or a modernization of the Ajanta style. Even in the West, Haas wrote, countries with great art traditions such as Italy or Spain have now only a few great artists. The reasons for this decline would be related to the historical and political decline of these countries. India's contemporary poverty in art lay in the fact that the mystically inspired life-element was outside the artist: 'Indian art shows the separation of the divine from the visible world, not their mutual interpenetration—even when it evokes the immanence of God in this world, and especially when it does so. All that lies beyond the here and now, all imaginary spaces and times are occupied in India by mythology and abstract theology' (Merkur 872).

The exclusion of the individual from a civilization like India meant for Haas that all modernity was either a superimposition or a juxtaposition, but not unification; modern dams and an age-old system of ploughing the fields or primitive animism and abstract, even atheistic and nihilistic philosophy. Modernity in India merely meant that India was a palimpsest. It is not surprising that Haas ends his brief meditation on art with a political reflection. In India space and time did not build a continuum. In India, time was without perspective, space without eternity, and nothing changed, nothing developed. Even historical time required an imaginary dimension in order to move: 'The real historical events appear strange and unconnected in this unhistorical country and we are observing—not without a measure of anxiety—a new political formation, which will probably not achieve anything other than to put a new layer of hyper-modern formations over the old stratified ones without establishing any connections between the two' (Merkur 872).

Nothing could be simpler than to see in Haas' formulations a variation of an essentialist dichotomization of cultures. He freely uses the familiar topoi of the European imagination of India so well analysed by critiques of orientalism. But Haas was not a theoretician of culture. His idealistic background made a comprehension of cultural complexity difficult. This is, however, a puzzling fact. The cultural complexity of the Danube monarchy should have sensitized him to the complexities of a colonial society rooted in tradition, yet struggling to overthrow colonialism and attempting to embark on a journey of modernity, however problematic that may have been.

It is precisely, however, because simple identification is not possible (in the sense of a naïve acceptance), and rejection is not permissible, that a logic of 'difference' has to be erected. In the case of Willy Haas this logic of difference has neither voyeuristic overtones, nor is it by any stretch of imagination the product of a colonial impulse. Haas consciously situated himself as a German-speaking Jew, living in exile, and in exile reacting to Fascism and trying to make his contribution to the anti-Fascist struggle. This, for him was the primary focus and it is, therefore, not surprising that his feelings for the British were marked by the gratitude of the refugee: 'They saved me from the German concentration camps, from the gas-chambers and the gallows, where almost all my relatives and friends, Czechs, Jews and German aristocrats died, unless they had committed suicide in time. How can I not be thankful to them for the rest of my life?' (LW 203).

But Haas did register certain aspects of the Indian freedom struggle: Indian antipathy to the British, anti-British propaganda, political boycott, and when, in a conversation, Bhavnani, his boss, coolly suggested that just as Haas hated Hitler, so too, Indians hated the British, Haas ended the passage with the comment 'Das war alles' (LW 264). Of course that was not all that could be said. Haas did mention that Indian soldiers were fighting the Japanese and that Gandhi reportedly spent sleepless nights at the thought of bombs over London. But the complex relation between the Indian contribution to the anti-Fascist struggle and the struggle for independence also explained Haas' ambivalences. 'Whatever we say about free India—and naturally we are on its side—at that time the white official was the last hope of the desperate Indian. He wasn't corrupt like the village headman, the village policeman. . . . This was the only "authority" that the rural Indian knew in daily life' (LW 215).

The problem for the contemporary reader may lie in the parentheses used by Haes; in the need to assure the reader that though, in humanistic terms, one has to support the desire of a country to be independent, there is, nevertheless, sufficient evidence to reclaim for the colonial power that measure of impartial justice which the native power structure lacked. This is a point of view which is perfectly consistent with many liberal European (and often also Indian) positions towards the anti-colonial struggles and the process of decolonization.

Haas wrote about India with a sense of urgency and troubled empathy. Perhaps the stylized cultural bracket he used to link cultural myths of Prague and India brings out this aspect clearly:

> I have never seen any miracles in India—not even the famous rope trick of the charmers. But I become serious when one calls India the 'land of miracles'. One is closer there to fate (Schicksal) than elsewhere. There are countries and places without fate. One can feel it. . . . But there are countries where the hand of fate reaches down to you, albeit in a curious manner. One such place is Prague. But the country of such countries is India. (LW 261)

The biennale in Venice, which Haas visited as a press correspondent, also gave him the opportunity to visit Padua where the sepulchre of St. Antony is situated. Indian readers will sympathize with the story he communicated. Apparently all one's wishes are fulfilled when one touches the marble of the sepulchre. Haas joined the chain of pilgrims and wished for a journey to India, the country of his childhood dreams.[11] He could not have known then that he would spend almost eight years there and that it would become a country he would, as he wrote 'love with an ache' (NR 88).

The gesture of a non-verbal epiphany is re-affirmed in his reaction to the news of Gandhi's assassination and these lines may perhaps be the closest approximation of his wish to articulate his Indian experience: 'Mahatma Gandhi, the great holy man of India was dead. I sat beside the radio in London and I knew suddenly that I would never understand this country, not the country and not its people. But I could love it. I still love it today. Perhaps this love is a higher kind of understanding which however cannot be expressed in words' (LW 267).

## NOTES AND REFERENCES

1. I am grateful to Dr Herta Haas, Hamburg, for much of the material on Willy Haas that I have used in this paper. I thank Rekha Kamath for commenting on an earlier draft and translating the quotes from the original German. *Die Literarische Welt* was reprinted as a facsimile edition by the 'Freie Akademie der Künste in Hamburg', ed. by Rolf Italiaander, 1961. For Haas' role in cinematographic history see 'Willy Haas. Der Kritiker als Mitproduzent', in *Texte zum Film, 1920-1933*, ed. by Wolfgang Jacobsen, Karl Prümm und Benno Wenz, Berlin, 1991 (edition Hentrich).
2. Cf. 'Career of Mr. Vilem Haas', (typed manuscript in the possession of Dr Herta Haas). This document was apparently required by Haas for his residential formalities in India. During his exile in India Haas used the Czech version 'Vilem' of his name 'Willy' (occasionally also 'Willi'). See also Luisa Valentini: *Willy Haas. Der Zeuge einer Epoche*. Frankfurt a.M., Peter Lang Verlag, 1983; Johannes H. Voigt, 'Die Emigration von Juden aus Mitteleuropa nach Indien während der Verfolgung durch das NS-Regime', in *Wechselwirkungen. Jahrbuch 1991. Aus Lehre und Forschung der Universität Stuttgart*.
3. Willy Haas, *Die Literarische Welt, Lebenserinnerungen*. München: Paul List Verlag, 1957. Republished Hamburg: Fischer Taschenbuch Verlag, 1983. I quote subsequently in the text from the 1983 edition as LW and page number.
4. Cf. Werner Vordtriede, 'Vorläufige Gedanken über eine Typologie der Exilliteratur', in *Akzente*, Vol. 15 (1968). Anna Seghers' novel *Transit* and Brecht's poems during the period 1933-45 bring out the problems of exile most vividly.
5. Erich Lüth, 'Wie Willy Haas (1891-73). deutscher Staatsbürger wurde', in *Jahrbuch. Freie Akademie der Künste in Hamburg*, 1974.
6. The composer Walter Kaufmann (1907-84), left Prague for India in 1934. He lived tor twelve years in Bombay and worked in the music department of All India Radio and also did significant research into Indian music. The signature tune of All India Radio, familiar to all Indian Radio listeners, was composed by him. Kaufmann later worked as conductor and teacher in Canada and USA. Interest in his life and compositions has recently revived. Cf. Agata Schindler, 'Bühnenwerk als Schiffskarte nach Bombay', *Sudetendeutsches Musikinstitut*, Regensburg, 1996. Cf. also Agata Schinder's contribution to the present volume.
7. Cf. 'Career of Mr Vilem Haas', op. cit.
8. *Germans Beyond Germany: An Anthology*. Edited, with biographical notes, and an Introduction by Vilem Haas, Bombay: The International Book House, 1942; V. Haas, 'On Teaching German Literature', in

*The Punjab Educational Journal*, Vol. XXXIX, September 1944, no. 6, October 1944, no. 7 and Vol. XLI, July 1945, no. 4; Vilem Haas, 'Franz Kafka', in *Tomorrow 1,* ed. by Raja Rao and Ahmed Ali, Bombay: Padma Publication, 1943. This essay may well be the first publication on Kafka in India; Vilem Haas, 'The Problem of the German Jews in Exile', in *The Indian Review*, Vol. XLI, no. 10, Madras, October 1940. *The Aryan Path,* Vol. XII, no. 6, June 1941, published a discussion on 'Hindu Widows' in which Vilem Haas and Radhakamal Mukherjee presented what the editor of the journal called the 'Western' and the 'Indian' point of view. A full bibliography of Haas' publications in India is unfortunately not available and would be desirable in the context of a history of exile in India. Karin Sandfort-Osterwald, *Willy Haas*, Eingeleitet von Rolf Italiaander, Hamburg: Hans Christians Verlag, 1969 (Hamburger Bibliographien Bd. 8) omits the period 1933-52.

9. Willi (*sic*) Haas, 'Indische Probleme', in *Neue Rundschau* (Stockholm: Bermann Fischer Verlag), October 1946, p. 85. Subsequently quoted in the text as NR and page number.
10. Willy Haas, 'Versuch über die indische Kunst', in *Merkur*, no. 43, 1951, p. 866. Subsequently quoted as Merkur and page number. The essay is reproduced in a slightly abridged version in LW, 303-12. Haas often uses the same material in different contexts and different writings on India.
11. Quoted from Willy Haas, 'Der Kritiker als Mitproduzent', op. cit. (note 1), p. 260. The editors of this volume refer to Rolf Italiaander, 'Erlebte Literaturgeschichte. Zum 65. Geburtstag von Willy Haas', in *Der Schriftsteller*, Heft 7/8, Sonderdruck, 1956.

5. Willy Haas on the 'Conte Rosso' when leaving Europe for India.

6. Willy Haas in Bhavnani's film studio in Bombay, 1940.

7. Front of Willy Haas' book *Germans Beyond Germany*, publ. Bombay, 1942.

8. Willy Haas as an officer of the British Indian Army during the Second World War.

# Alex Aronson: Refugee from Nazi Germany in Santiniketan[1]

*Martin Kämpchen*

## SANTINIKETAN AND NATIONAL SOCIALISM

Initially, I was asked to write a paper on Central European refugees who were victims of Nazism and who had come to Santiniketan. This subject was chosen with the assumption that Rabindranath Tagore's 'abode of peace', with its ideal of international brotherhood, would be a natural haven for Central European Jews. The ashram had accepted scholars and social workers from Europe and America from the 1920s onward. They were attracted to Tagore and his ideal of building an international educational centre through their contact with the poet during his extensive lecture tours abroad. It is true that Santiniketan did receive many foreign visitors; however, they generally arrived to witness or cooperate in the educational efforts for which the place became well-known, or merely to have Tagore's *darshan*. They were never people in distress, never politically persecuted.

So, when I searched the archives of Rabindra-Bhavan in Santiniketan for material on refugees fleeing from the scourge of National Socialism, I found very little. Even the young German Jew, Alex Aronson (who was eventually to settle in Santiniketan), did not flee Nazi terror directly from Germany. Instead, he left Germany in 1933 to continue his education in France and Great Britain. After obtaining a B.A. degree in English literature from Cambridge, he opted against returning to Germany and applied to the Visva-Bharati University for a lectureship. Aronson joined the ashram more in the capacity of a teacher than as a refugee. Yet, once in India, the war forced him to remain in this relatively safe country until its end.

A perusal of *Visva-Bharati News*, the monthly news bulletin of the university, does not bring to light a single European refugee finding shelter in Santiniketan. The correspondence files at Rabindra-Bhavan reveal only two genuine cases in which politically persecuted Germans tried to find refuge at Santiniketan. One correspondent, Guenther Droesse, begins his letter with these words: 'As I am [only] half-Aryan, I cannot work in Germany under the present regime anymore, although I had an occupation at the "Waldorf-School". As I have a predilection for the East, especially for India, I want to ask you, if you could perhaps do something for me, to find a post as a teacher. . . .'[2] The reply, written by the Secretary to Rabindranath Tagore, ignores Droesse's political predicament and merely states: 'Dr Tagore has been much touched by your letter. . . . He is very sorry he is not in a position to do anything for you.'[3]

The second letter was sent from Turkey by a German professor of astronomy, E. Finlay-Freundlich, who had to leave his country 'where brutal power had become the only idol worth worshipping'. He, in turn, sent this letter to India with a 'young friend' who was 'unable to live [any] longer in the Germany of today', requesting Tagore to help him. His fate is not known.[4] But there must have been other requests of a similar nature. I am, for example, aware of two letters to C.F. Andrews, written by Alex Aronson himself during the war, interceding on behalf of two Jewish immigrants who were stranded in India.[5]

Did Hitler's Nazism, the Second World War and the near extermination of a whole people pass by the 'abode of peace' unnoticed? Were these catastrophes too remote to be imagined and find a suitable reaction by the Tagorean aesthetic world-view and lifestyle? If we take the two journals published from Visva-Bharati, the *Visva-Bharati News* and the *Visva-Bharati Quarterly*, as indicators, it may almost seem so. In neither journal does the war in Europe and the ensuing major changes on the international scene figure prominently. Naturally, if current affairs played a role at all, what did receive attention was the plight of the Indian people struggling for her political independence, cultural identity and spiritual dignity. The political situation of Europe was, indeed, quite far away.

Yet, this is only one side of the picture. As early as August 1933, a significant small paragraph was included in an essay, entitled 'Santiniketan: A Dream'.[6] The author, Krishna Kripalani, observes:

Sometimes I sit and dream on if Santiniketan had had the requisite financial strength, and if it had the daring to offer an asylum, with a moderate maintenance, to some of the great and noble Jewish scholars and writers, now rendered homeless in their birth-place, Santiniketan might have become an Abode, not only of Peace, but of benediction. But we have no funds:—our arms that might be outstretched have to hang down.[7]

This observation is an indication that the need to give shelter to Jewish refugees was felt and discussed among the ashramites. But financial constraints stood in the way of offering help.

The *Visva-Bharati News* was clearly on the side of the victims of war and racial violence when it published two letters describing the situation in Europe[8] and an essay by Marjorie Sykes entitled 'What has this War to do with Us?'[9] This excellent text exhorts the ashramites to dedicate themselves to non-violent service among the under-privileged and to refuse to be swayed by war propaganda.

Jewish contacts of a different kind were anticipated by Rabindranath Tagore when he, in 1937, invited members of a Zionist organization to come to India and establish small model farms near Sriniketan. He wanted them to introduce the novel farming techniques which they had successfully developed in Palestine. Tagore wrote to a certain Dr Immanuel Olsvanger that 'the inspiration that your workers can give us if some of them would join us here and start settlements of their own would be invaluable; their experience and example would, I feel sure, bring untold benefit both to our village organisers and to the villagers themselves'.[10]

Tagore went as far as to send an 'outline scheme for cooperation between Jewish pioneers and workers at Visva-Bharati'. Nothing, however, was heard of the scheme thereafter.

At the end of 1940, while the war was in progress, Rathindranath Tagore (son of Rabindranath) suggested to the rector of the Hebrew University at Jerusalem a 'scheme for increasing collaboration and interchange of scholars between Visvabharati' and that university.[11] Yet, he conceded, that they had to wait for 'peaceful times' before such a plan could be implemented. These were attempts to be in contact not with Jewish refugees but with Jews who had already settled in Palestine.

Only once was there a departure from this line of sober sympathy for the victims of Nazism, namely, when the 'Acting Consul-General of Germany in India', Dr Herbert Richter, delivered a speech to the students in Santiniketan, a summary of which was published in *Visva-Bharati News.*[12] Brazen propaganda for Hitler and the Third Reich was offered here, and there was obviously no one in Santiniketan who saw through this clever language and prevented, at least, the publication of the summary. This happened in the first year of Hitler's regime, when the newspapers in India were outspoken in their praise for Hitler.

The crucial question arises: What was Rabindranath Tagore's personal role in the denunciation of German Nazism? We recall that, in 1926, Tagore was able to surmount his reluctance to publicly denounce Benito Mussolini's Italian Fascism only after Romain Rolland's stern admonition. Regarding Nazism, there are a few letters in which he voiced his protest against Albert Einstein's mistreatment at the hands of the Nazis, a protest which found its way into newspapers. Yet this protest has a note of hesitation in it. Let me quote from a letter of 1934 to N.E.B. Ezra, editor of the *Israel Messenger*:

> As regards the Hitler regime in Germany, we read different versions of it. And certainly it cannot be denied that the German people were goaded to many acts of desperate folly by the humiliations imposed on them by the victorious nations of the War. Nevertheless, if the brutalities we read of are authentic, then no civilised conscience can allow compromise with them. The insults offered to my friend Einstein have shocked me to the point of torturing my faith in modern civilisation. I can only draw consolation from the hope that it was an unhappy act done in a drunken mood and not the sober choice of a people so gifted as the Germans.[13]

Naturally, it was hard for Tagore to accept that the very people who had showered praise and adulation on him a decade earlier, had now elected a government which was barbaric and racist. Tagore could have easily convinced himself, however, that Nazi barbarities were 'authentic' and not merely stray acts of 'folly' when a year earlier, in April 1933, his grandnephew Soumyendranath Tagore, was arrested at the German border under the suspicion of having plotted to assassinate Hitler. He was kept for several days in Munich and subjected to torture. He witnessed the horrifying treatment meted out to other prisoners. After his escape to Paris, Soumyendranath's report was carried by numerous newspapers.[14]

Some months afterwards, Soumyendranath read about Herbert Richter's lecture at Santiniketan which praised Hitler's Germany. He dispatched a furious, hard-hitting letter to his great-uncle Rabindranath accusing him of maintaining silence in the face of such provocation. People of all countries were up in arms against Hitler, he wrote, 'only you are silent. . . . They expected a protest from you. You have not seized upon the special opportunity which India has had.'[15] Rabindranath's reply to his young relative is unfortunately lost. In a short essay 'Kalantar', first published in the journal *Parichay* as early as August 1933,[16] Rabindranath, however, did denounce Fascism, including its German brand, in no uncertain terms. This was probably unknown to Soumyendranath. Again, at the time the war broke out in 1939, Rabindranath issued a strong statement to the press denouncing 'the arrogant unrighteousness of the present ruler of Germany'.[17]

## ALEX ARONSON'S LIFE IN EUROPE AND INDIA

I shall now briefly trace Alex Aronson's personal development from his childhood and youth in Europe until his years of exile in Santiniketan and Dhaka. I base this outline on his three published volumes of memoirs: *The Seeds of Time*,[18] which covers Aronson's life until his departure to India, *Brief Chronicles of the Time*,[19] which relate to his stay in Bengal from 1937 until 1946, and *For the Time Being*[20] offering a summing up of his life with an emphasis on his stay in Israel. All three volumes were, by the way, published in Calcutta—not in Israel or Germany. This factor is an indication as to where the author expected to find a larger number of interested readers, and in which country his life appears to have the greatest historical relevance. Further, I base this essay on the numerous letters I have received from Alex Aronson since April 1989.

In one of the last letters I received from Aronson before his death in December 1995, he seemed to spell out the overriding theme of his entire life wherever it was spent, in Europe, India or Israel. He wrote: 'I have been an alien and an exile wherever I went.'[21]

His journey through the years has been one through many countries, in none of which was he able to establish deep roots. His multicultural and multilingual existence was not something he chose consciously, coming to him instead through his family. He was born in 1912 in the city of Breslau which was then in German territory, though it is now situated in Poland. His parents were Russian and had emigrated to Germany because 'it represented a degree of civilization unknown in Russia. . . . Germany was the country of emancipation and progress.'[22] His father was a businessman. When the First World War erupted in 1914, Alex's father stayed on in Russia on business. His mother, 'threatened with internment as a Russian national, and responsible for the fate of two infants, had to escape back to Russia at the very last minute'.[23] The child Alex grew up amidst the chaos of war, crossing 'shifting and arbitrary frontiers', travelling 'from West to East and then back again from East to West according to the fortunes of war'.[24] Alex grew up speaking Russian and German, his 'two mother tongues'.[25] By virtue of their father's newly acquired passport, he and his brother became Lithuanian citizens without even knowing where Lithuania was situated!

'Linguistic schizophrenia'[26] became part of his life. He soon learned Latin, French and Hebrew from private teachers. Early on he discovered a passion for books, which would stay with him throughout his life. 'The German classics were our daily diet', he noted.[27] However, the classical literatures of other languages were soon added. In fact, reading the two volumes of Aronson's memoirs it almost appears as if his life has been lived more fully in the world of literature than in 'normal' reality. To this he added his multilingual attempts at lyrical writing. With a comical undertone, he confessed: 'Words rarely failed me. I was good at translating from German into French, and at a later date, from French into English. In France I wrote poetry in the German language. In England I wrote poetry in French, while during my stay in India I decided that English was the language of poetry I should use.'[28]

With the rise of Hitler, Alex Aronson, just a little over 20 years old, left Germany on 1 April 1933 and went to the south of France for further studies. He would never return to the country of his birth except in his old age on short visits. In Montpellier and Toulouse he studied French and comparative literature and wrote a doctoral thesis on 'Lessing et les Classiques Français'. With amusement Aronson remembers his stint as a youthful 'Monsieur le Directeur' of a Berlitz language school. Yet it was here that he for the first time came face to face with xenophobia and anti-Semitism.

On his father's request, Alex Aronson moved on to Cambridge to study English and thus added yet another language to his linguistic storehouse. When he had completed his studies with a B.A. in 1937, the political situation in Germany was such that it was inadvisable for him to return there. To find a job in Great Britain was difficult. Coincidence then intervened. Aronson remembers the exact date: It was on 11 February 1937 that he met a Chinese scholar who had recently arrived to study Shakespeare. This gentleman had stopped over in India and visited Tagore's Santiniketan. In Aronson's words: 'He raised his voice as if prophetically transported, and suggested that the Poet was only waiting for me to share his thoughts and emotions which . . . were recollected in that tranquillity which the West had lost long ago.'[29]

Aronson immediately wrote a letter to Rabindranath Tagore inquiring about a vacancy at his university. He recollects: 'I explained who I was, my academic standing, my status as a refugee from Nazi Germany, and hinted at my wish to serve and to share.'[30]

A few weeks later the poet's son, Rathindranath Tagore, replied offering Aronson a lectureship in English literature.[31] The letter also requested Aronson to get in touch with two close associates of Tagore, namely Amiya Chakravarty and C.F. Andrews who were staying in England at the time. Both men enlightened the young Aronson about Indian conditions warning him against idealized illusions; yet both suggested that he give it a try and go to India.

Alex Aronson, barely 25 years old, arrived in Santiniketan on 7 November 1937. Temperamentally, he always preferred 'a life of contemplation rather than action';[32] he was never tempted to participate in the political life of his time and of the country he lived in. In Santiniketan he found a place which provided him 'a shelter from chaos and disintegration',[33] from the political and social turmoil of Europe and India alike. It was a place which provided not only basic physical comfort but also emotional and spiritual succour. Besides, it created for him an ideal setting for hard and creative work as a teacher, researcher and academic writer. The 'unreality' of life at Santiniketan led him sometimes to almost forget the hardships which his people in Europe had to bear. This discrepancy between his own relative comfort and the brutality and insanity in the world outside has, for Aronson, always been a cause of anguish and self-doubt.

In his letters and published writings Aronson never tired of expressing his gratitude for the warm treatment he received at Santiniketan: 'The hospitality I received there goes beyond all praise. It is something I shall never forget and for which I shall be for ever grateful.'[34]

Alex Aronson adjusted well amidst the ashram milieu, wearing Indian style clothes and eating, for the first two years, Indian food from the general kitchen. He was at the centre of activity, as he insists, and did not feel treated like a foreigner.[35] With youthful enthusiasm, he applied his mind towards understanding and adjusting to his new environment. He tried to read his way into the Eastern mind, studying Indian philosophy and art, hoping to gauge the differences between what was 'Western' and what was 'Eastern'. A fair number of essays and reviews which began to appear in Visva-Bharati periodicals and elsewhere in India testify to his seriousness.

Yet, very early on, it also became inescapably clear to him that he was and would remain essentially a European: 'My future, surely, lay in the West, in the company of Shakespeare and Mozart, not in what appeared to me the chaotic East with its intellectual muddle, its contradictory mythologies of celestial good and sublunary evil, its alien and manyheaded gods and luscious goddesses.'[36]

Aronson enjoyed playing the piano and listening to gramophone records together with Satyajit Ray, who was then an art student in Santiniketan. Aronson's aesthetic and intellectual concerns were, however, primarily European. His inability to learn Bengali in order to communicate with the people around him in their mother tongue is perhaps an indication of his intense preoccupation with himself and his fate as a European refugee. Instead he preferred to delve into English literature.[37]

Aronson soon became keenly aware that the Utopia of Santiniketan was riddled with human imperfections. What else could be expected? Only Rabindranath Tagore was truly impressive and outstanding. With fondness he remembers in his memoirs his various encounters with the poet:

> I met Tagore a number of times. We talked about the teaching of English poetry to the students. I recall how deeply impressed I was by his voice, his physical appearance, the utter simplicity of his arguments which were less literary than human. I listened without interrupting him. I was, naturally, much too intimidated to contradict or to argue. That first interview lasted half an hour. By the time I left his room darkness had fallen. I was as if intoxicated by the warmth of his voice, the shape of his hands, the sensuous perfection of his face.[38]

The people around Tagore proved to be well-meaning but average. In a letter Aronson explains his viewpoint:

> The people surrounding [Tagore] were mostly . . . quite unable to respond to his greatness, ineffectual except in bureaucratic matters, fit only to keep undesirable visitors from his room and organise his timetable. This, I believe, was inevitable and followed a pattern which is the natural result of the impossible synthesis of genius and commonplace people. From the day I arrived at S[antiniketan] to the last day I was aware of this discrepancy and took it for granted.[39]

Of the people around Rabindranath, Aronson probably was closest to Krishna Kripalani with whom he also enjoyed some intellectual cooperation. Aronson met C.F. Andrews only 'a couple of times' in Santiniketan shortly before the latter's death. Amiya Chakravarty he describes as 'a grey eminence . . ., invisible but ever present', and the poet's son, Rathindranath Tagore, he remembers best as 'an avid bridge player': 'His was a remote presence, rarely seen except as a distant spectrelike figure, though much in evidence as the head of the institution.'[40]

As a teacher 'Aron-*da*' ('elder brother Aron')—as he was affectionately called by his students—did not derive the 'intellectual challenge' he expected and wanted;[41] his students, though eager to learn from their foreign master, had no serious academic aspirations. Aronson taught English literature at Visva-Bharati University, preparing his students for the B.A. examination of Calcutta University. He must have created a profound impression on the mind of many of his students. Even half a century later, a large number of people in Santiniketan remember their former teacher fondly.

After Tagore's death, Aronson stayed on in Santiniketan for another three years. In July/August 1944, he accepted a vacancy in the English Department of Dhaka University. There he was very welcome as 'a teacher who had come to them straight from the Abode of Peace'.[42] The students in Dhaka were of a different mettle, not the dreamy, poetry-writing kind of Santiniketan, but 'pragmatic', alive to social concerns, 'politically alert', 'aggressively articulate' and 'intellectually impatient'.[43]

Soon after the war, Aronson realized that he was homesick, and the 'need to return to what I considered to be my real home, Palestine, the country where my family had settled and built a new life'[44] became more and more urgent. In 1946, after having spent two years at Dhaka, he returned to his family, completing an exile of almost nine years.

## ALEX ARONSON'S ACADEMIC ACHIEVEMENTS DURING EXILE

The contemplative, leisurely atmosphere of Santiniketan has been the undoing of many fine academic minds that have declined into lethargy and complacency there. A few others have been able to harness the absence of any daunting obstacles to daily life for a career of enormous productivity. Alex Aronson has been among these few; he was able to work well in Santiniketan.[45] Arriving as a young man in 1937, with, by his own admission,[46] an as yet insufficient knowledge of English, he wrote within the nine years of exile three books, published in India, while editing two others, one of which was also published. Further, I have counted fourteen essays, many exceeding two dozen pages, and six book reviews in the two journals published from the University at Santiniketan, namely, the *Visva-Bharati News* and *Visva-Bharati Quarterly*. In addition, there are two long essays in the *Santiniketan Sammelani Magazine*. He also wrote articles for journals published outside Santiniketan, namely, in the famous *Modern Review* (Calcutta), in *The Calcutta Review* (Calcutta University), *The Twentieth Century* (Allahabad), besides in the literary supplements of various English, Bengali and Hindi newspapers.[47] The sheer quantity of academic output is amazing, especially for a man so young as Aronson was.

Let us also try to assess the quality of his academic writing. In his essays, the author surveys an impressive panorama of themes and subjects. He discusses contemporary French poetry, problems of education, of poetics, of literature and psychology; he writes on Dostoevsky and, of course, Rabindranath Tagore. These essays already revealed his predilection for comparative themes which would dominate the scholarly books Aronson was to write later in his life. Consider some titles of his early essays: 'Literature and Social Environment', 'Poetry and the Analysis of the Ego', 'Rabindranath and Western Music'. Besides these essays, he published a long poem distinctly religious in mood[48] and the translation of a short story by Rainer Maria Rilke.[49]

The first, and probably most important book he wrote at Santiniketan was his *Rabindranath through Western Eyes*, published in 1943.[50] There is a story behind this book which Aronson relates in his memoirs. Rathindranath Tagore, the poet's son, asked Aronson to 'introduce some sort of order into the Tagore archive'[51] consisting of some 'sixty files of newspaper cuttings'[52] and numerous files of correspondence containing 'thousands of letters addressed to Tagore'.[53] During the course of many months of hard, single-minded work, Aronson classified these newspaper articles and letters and thus laid the basis for the present archive at Rabindra-Bhavan. Aronson was jubilant: 'This extraordinary collection . . . seemed to me, in effect, the dream come true of every scholar whose concern is with the varieties of literary response evoked by a man of genius among his contemporaries.'[54]

Many newspaper articles dealt with Tagore's visits to Europe and America. Delighted with this 'wealth of information',[55] Aronson not only gave order to this material, but also—'in a frenzy of discovery'[56]—he wrote a book on the Western responses to Tagore based on these newspaper clippings. He consciously focused on the popular response as expressed through the daily press, rather than on the sophisticated responses of scholars, writers and intellectuals. With the help of this focus, Aronson was able to explore the social climate in which the shallow and largely misguided popular enthusiasm for Tagore could grow, and thus he developed his book into a study of the origins of cultural attitudes. Aronson clarified in a letter:

[The book] I wanted to write [was] not about Tagore (my ignorance of Bengali disqualified me from such an undertaking), but about the West: its reaction to a great poet who had come to them from the East, the Western response to India at that time (mainly between 1920 and 1935). . . . I considered the book a novel approach to literary criticism, not in terms of sentimental hero-worship (to which Indians are particularly given), but in terms of critical (or uncritical) response. That such a response, especially during these fateful years, was coloured by social, political and religious prejudices opened my eyes to possibilities of reappraisal which shocked some Indians but was accepted enthusiastically by the younger generation.[57]

The book *Rabindranath through Western Eyes* received a devastating review from Amal Home in the *Visva-Bharati Quarterly*[58] accusing its author of 'bias and preconceived notions'[59] against Tagore and the admirers of Tagore in the West. Many members of the Santiniketan establishment presumably shared this view. So did Amiya Chakravarty who contributed a preface to the book. While a preface is traditionally meant to win sympathy and understanding for a book, Chakravarty criticized Aronson's book to such an extent that he, towards the end, had to give a twist to his text: 'The introductory criticisms, paradoxically enough, must be accepted as evidence of this writer's appreciation of Dr Aronson's book.'[60] Paradoxical, indeed!

Home and Chakravarty had clearly misunderstood Aronson's intentions, who had never meant to malign the poet. Home's scathing remarks must have deeply hurt the young scholar who once admitted that they indeed contributed to his decision to leave Santiniketan.[61]

The second fruit of Aronson's many months of research among these cuttings and correspondences was his manuscript 'Letter to a Poet' which compiled 95 letters to Tagore written by well-known writers, scholars and public personalities from Europe and America, complete with an 'Introduction' and 'notes' on each letter.[62] These letters, according to the 'Introduction', 'unfold before our eyes the history of Europe during the last forty years, and they reveal to us all that was great and significant in Rabindranath Tagore's life.'[63]

This manuscript could not be published because of 'copyright difficulties during the war'. Aronson further commented: 'I also had the impression that Rathindranath did not wish these letters to be published by a non-Indian and non-Bengali.'[64]

Romain Rolland must have been a model for the young Alex Aronson, because this French writer, though steeped in European culture, was actively interested in things Indian and attempted in his life and in his writings to combine his Europeanness with what he considered valuable in India. Aronson's book, *Romain Rolland: The Story of a Conscience*,[65] was (according to Krishna Kripalani) the first book in the English language on Rolland's work as a writer, pacifist and interpreter of Eastern thought since the English translation of Stefan Zweig's account of Rolland's life written two decades earlier.[66] In the chapter 'Knowledge of the East',[67] Aronson, drawing from his own experience of India, summarizes at some length Rolland's study of the Indian personalities such as Ramakrishna, Swami Vivekananda and Mahatma Gandhi.

An offshoot of this full-blown study of Rolland was the book *Rolland and Tagore*[68] which Aronson edited jointly with Krishna Kripalani. This book brings together Rolland's letters to Tagore as well as the essays these two personalities wrote about each other. The publication of these two books on this pacifist and internationalist towards the end of the Second World War was especially timely.

The last book to be published shortly before leaving his exile was Aronson's *Europe looks at India: A Study in Cultural Relations*.[69] While the four books mentioned earlier are built around Tagore and Rolland, the last volume opens a wider perspective allowing the reader to have an overview of the cultural relations between Europe and India during the last 150 years. Aronson's knowledge of several European languages serves him well as he discusses French writers like Voltaire, Romain Rolland and Réne Guénon, German writers and philosophers like Goethe and the Romantics, Hegel, Schopenhauer, Nietzsche, Spengler and Count Hermann Keyserling, and English-language writers like Emerson, Yeats, D.H.Lawrence and Aldous Huxley. This, to my knowledge, is the first book dealing with the European cultural response to India comprehensively. Since then many other studies have followed, none of which, I believe, refers to this pioneering venture. This is a book in need of resurrection.

Considering the achievements of these five books, what astonishes me most is the enormously wide range of reading which the young Alex Aronson was able to draw on. His judgements reveal insights into the cultural developments of Europe normally associated with a person several decades his senior. His judgements are uttered with astonishing self-confidence and ease. He is never afraid to criticize and even reject, but his tone, though firm, is devoid of any shrillness or extreme views. His English, a language he had learned a few years earlier, never lacks in sophistication of expression and discipline of thought.

## ALEX ARONSON'S INTERNMENT

With the outbreak of the Second World War, Aronson, a German national, was technically an enemy alien in India even though he, being a Jew, could not be suspected of giving allegiance to Nazi ideology. Like many other Jewish refugees, Aronson volunteered his 'service to the British war effort' but was told that only doctors and nurses 'could be of use'.[70] Aronson was also in touch with the Calcutta office of the Jewish Relief Association, run by local Jewish people, who were mostly of British origin.

On the day war was declared, a police officer came to remove him from the ashram, taking him to Fort William in Calcutta. Outraged and full of indignation, he described his situation in letters sent to Santiniketan. Here is an excerpt, reproduced in the *Visva-Bharati News:*

> My position here is preposterous and unbearable. I have suffered so many humiliations at the hands of the German Nazis and yet I am detained with a whole crowd of them. I have lost my German citizenship years ago[71] and yet I am here . . . I am grateful to the officers of this Camp who make the best of a bad job. But this is obviously not my place in India. It is for the first time since seven years that I've to live in intimate contact with Germans. This is more than what any civilised person would bear.[72]

His *Brief Chronicles of the Time* devotes one chapter to his experience in the internment camp. He was lodged in one of the tents together with about 200 occupants; among them were 'some sixty or seventy members of the Nazi party'.[73] From Fort William the camp was soon shifted to Ahmednagar. There a government committee was formed, headed by Malcolm Darling, to investigate each case. Within two days of Darling interrogating Alex Aronson, the latter was released and allowed to return to Santiniketan. None the less, he had spent a little over two months[74] behind barbed wires.

A year later, in mid-1940, Aronson was again threatened with internment. He repeatedly received letters from the government informing him that he would be sent to a parole settlement in the near future.[75] In order to ward off this imminent danger, Rabindranath Tagore personally wrote a three-page letter (on 4 August 1940), to Sir Reginald M. Maxwell, the Home Member of the Government of India, Simla, interceding on Aronson's behalf, who, as Tagore emphasized was ' a valuable member of the staff of the Visva-Bharati and it will be difficult to replace him'.[76] Tagore elaborately explained Aronson's somewhat complex nationality status, the circumstances by which he, a German Jew, had come to India, and then cited several of Aronson's former British teachers at Cambridge all of whom 'testified to Dr Aronson's personality, character and expressed high regard for him'. Obviously, the opinions of these fellow Englishmen were expected to weigh more in Maxwell's eyes than those of the Nobel laureate Rabindranath Tagore. So he only added, rather meekly, that 'the impression Dr Aronson produced in Cambridge he has repeated here amongst us'.

Maxwell's reply, dated 19 August 1940, was short and dry: 'The position in regard to Dr Aronson is that he is being sent to a parole settlement in pursuance of the general policy which is now being followed.' But Tagore was assured that if these 'precautions' could be relaxed, his 'strong representations on behalf of Dr Aronson will be given full weight'.[77]

By no means satisfied with this reply, Tagore next interceded on behalf of Aronson to Khwaja Sir Nazimuddin, an influential member of the government in undivided Bengal and a future prime minister of Pakistan.[78] Obviously Tagore's efforts had not been in vain, because a few weeks later Aronson was informed that his being sent to parole settlement had been 'indefinitely postponed'.[79]

It is only natural that internment and its aftermath imbued the young Alex Aronson, who was a mere 27 years old at that time, with a deep sense of insecurity regarding his own life and the life of the Jewish people in Europe. Even though he was able to survive the war unscathed in remote Santiniketan, news about the progress of the war did reach him and filled him with horror and anguish. Besides, a Japanese invasion of Bengal was imminent; paratroopers were expected to descend any day. Meanwhile, his colleagues and students at

Santiniketan showed more interest in singing their songs and, at best, reflecting about their country's liberation from British rule. I quote from one of Aronson s letters to C.F. Andrews, written soon after his release from the internment camp:

The question, dear Mr Andrews, is no longer whether it will be possible to save the Jewish Civilization, but whether the Jewish people as such have any home left to survive this cataclysm. Whether apart from Palestine which after all is an infinitely small country, my people will be a people of refugees uprooted, demoralized, and disassociated with their past and their future, whether those cargo-boats loaded with refugees will one day stop crossing the seas and indeed find an abode of peace, whether there will be leaders enough to guide us out of this universal Egypt of ours. . . .[80]

## ARONSON'S LIFE IN ISRAEL

Alex Aronson's memoirs, *Brief Chronicles of the Time*, end with his departure from India and arrival in Palestine: 'I had arrived home. At last, I thought, I had left exile behind.'[81]

He joined his mother—his father having expired just a few weeks earlier—and his brother. At least he had the consolation of living with his family. Indeed, in Palestine, which soon after became the state of Israel, Alex Aronson spent the major part of his lifespan of 82 years. The third part of his memoirs relates the story of his life in Israel.

At Santiniketan he had begun teaching. In Israel he made teaching his lifelong profession and, indeed, passion. He felt that the knowledge and experience he had accumulated during his sojourns in France, England and India 'could only be realised in the teaching profession'.[82] Over the years he has become one of the best-known and most revered university teachers in Israel.[83]

He was initially a guest lecturer at the Hebrew University in Jerusalem for a year and then a teacher in a secondary school in Tel-Aviv for several years. Next he received a lectureship at the University of Tel-Aviv. As a professor emeritus in Haifa he gave classes at the university until shortly before his death on 10 December 1995. Having never married, he lived alone. But his brother and sister-in-law stayed a mere stone's throw away; their adult children and families live near Haifa.

Alex Aronson, being an indefatigable letter writer, had kept in touch with numerous contemporaries in Santiniketan and Calcutta, most of whom have died in the meantime. He continued to write on Tagore, especially several essays about the poet's educational ideas. Only once, in 1980, had Aronson revisited India; his impressions are collected in verse in *India Revisited*,[84] a section of the one volume of poetry he published. Thereafter several other invitations could not lure him back to his 'second home', not even the honorary doctorate of literature (Desikottama) which the Visva-Bharati University of Santiniketan awarded him in 1993 *in absentia*. More than the discomfort of the journey, he feared confronting the fact that most of his friends had died and hardly anybody was left with whom he could exchange memories.[85]

His exile in Santiniketan continued to be, as he confessed, 'that part of my life which I most vividly remember'.[86] Personally as well as professionally, his years as a refugee were an early climax in his life. It took over a quarter of a century until Aronson's next books of literary criticism began to be published. Some of them deal with that literary giant to whom he devoted so much of his energy as a teacher and academic writer: William Shakespeare.

Although he remained in close touch with numerous former colleagues and students through correspondence, telephone calls and visits, Professor Alex Aronson basically continued to follow the retiring life of intellectual contemplation which he had led in Santiniketan. Uninspired by political issues, by temperament not a social activist, Aronson lived in Israel in silent disagreement with his surroundings. A few sentences from a letter sum up his life in Israel succinctly: 'I was never a fanatic Zionist nor an orthodox Jew. Opposed as I am to any form of nationalism and being a pacifist by conviction and temperament I hardly ever found a suitable place in this country. On the other hand I couldn't possibly live anywhere else. Unwilling to adapt myself to the political life of this or any other country, I am by definition an outsider.'[87]

## NOTES

1. I thank Uma Das Gupta, Supriya Roy, Sutapa Bhattacharya, Andrew Robinson and Rick Ross for their help with this essay. My deepest debt of gratitude I owe, of course, to Professor Alex Aronson.

   In the following, these abbreviations are used: RBh (Rabindra-Bhavan archives, Santiniketan); *VBN* (*Visva-Bharati News*, Santiniketan); *VBQ* (*Visva-Bharati Quarterly*, Santiniketan).

2. Letter dated 4 April 1934 (RBh).
3. Letter dated 26 April 1934 (RBh).
4. Letter dated 5 November 1936, sent from Istanbul (RBh).
5. Private archive of Alex Aronson, Haifa. Letters dated 12 November 1939 and 20 November 1939, written from Santiniketan. C.F. Andrews' reply, dated 16 November 1939, was written from Ahmedabad.
6. VBN, August 1933, pp. 12f.
7. Ibid., p. 13.
8. C.F. Andrews: 'A Letter' [to Rabindranath Tagore]. *VBN*, October 1938, pp. 28f.; the extract of a letter 'written by an American friend' to Rathindranath Tagore, dated 2 April 1939. *VBN*, May 1939, p. 86.
9. *VBN*, October 1939, pp. 27-9.
10. Letter dated 8 July 1937 (RBh).
11. Letter dated 12 December 1940 (RBh).
12. Dr Herbert Richter, 'The Situation in Germany', in *VBN*, September 1933, pp. 19f. The lecture was held on 12 August 1933.
13. Exact date of letter not given (RBh).
14. Soumyendranath Tagore collected his articles on German Fascism in his book *Hitlerism: The Aryan Rule in Germany*, Calcutta: n.d. (the dedication is dated December 1933). This book also includes the author's report of his arrest in Germany ('A Sample of Hitler's National Germany', pp. 83-94).
15. This letter of 1 November 1933 is reproduced in Nepal Majumdar, *Rabindranath: Kayekti Rajnitik Prasanga*, Calcutta: Cirayat Prakasan, 1987, pp. 97-100. Quotation translated by the author. Andrew Robinson (London) has provided me with material on this problem. See also Krishna Dutta/Andrew Robinson, *Rabindranath Tagore: The Myriad-Minded Man*, London: Bloomsbury, 1995, pp. 343f.
16. Sraban 1340. See Majumdar, op. cit., pp. 105f.
17. *Modern Review* (Calcutta), October 1939, p. 378. See also the chapter 'Tagore on Fascism', pp. 3-18, in *Anti-Fascist Traditions of Bengal: An Anthology in Celebration of the 20th Anniversary of the Foundation of the German Democratic Republic*, compiled and published by Indo-GDR Friendship Society, Calcutta: n.d. [1969].
18. Alex Aronson, *The Seeds of Time*, Calcutta: Writers Workshop, 1994.
19. Alex Aronson, *Brief Chronicles of the Time*, Calcutta : Writers Workshop, 1990.
20. Alex Aronson, *For the Time Being*, Calcutta : Writers Workshop, 1995.
21. Letter to Martin Kämpchen (Santiniketan), dated 9 February1995.
22. Aronson, *The Seeds of Time*, p. 27.
23. Ibid. p. 25.
24. Ibid.
25. Ibid., p. 32.

26. Ibid.
27. Ibid., p. 35.
28. Ibid., pp. 44f.
29. Aronson, *Brief Chronicles of the Time*, p. 18.
30. Ibid.
31. Besides following the narrative of *Brief Chronicles of the Time*, I use from this point also Dr Uma Das Gupta's notes of an interview with Aronson in 1980. Dr Das Gupta (Calcutta) has kindly allowed me to use them.
32. Aronson, *The Seeds of the Time*, p. 57.
33. Letter to Martin Kämpchen, dated 30 April 1989.
34. Ibid.
35. See Dr Uma Das Gupta's notes.
36. Aronson, *Brief Chronicles of the Time*, p. 33.
37. See ibid., p. 95.
38. Aronson, *For the Time Being*, p. 49; from 'I listened . . .' I follow the manuscript of this third volume of memoirs, pp. 15f. This passage was subsequently deleted for print.
39. Letter to Krishna Dutta (London), dated 20 January 1993.
40. Letter to Martin Kämpchen, dated 22 April 1995.
41. Aronson, *Brief Chronicles of the Time*, p. 95.
42. Ibid., p. 106.
43. Ibid.
44. Ibid., p. 109. Alex Aronson's parents emigrated from Germany to Palestine in September 1933.
45. See also Dr Uma Das Gupta's notes.
46. 'I still had to overcome my deficiencies in English before trying to acquire Bengali or Hindi' (Aronson, *Brief Chronicles of the Time*, p. 95).
47. Letter to Martin Kämpchen, dated 22 April 1995.
48. Alex Aronson, 'Before the Sun Rises', *VBQ*, November 1940, pp. 260-4.
49. Alex Aronson, 'An Association Born of an Urgent Need', *VBQ*, May-July 1944, pp. 17-34.
50. Alex Aronson, *Rabindranath through Western Eyes*, Allahabad: Kitabistan, 1943; republished Calcutta: Riddhi-India, 1978.
51. Aronson, *Brief Chronicles of the Time*, p. 55.
52. Ibid., p. 56
53. Ibid., p. 55.
54. Ibid., p. 56.
55. Ibid., p. 57.
56. Ibid., p. 58.
57. Letter to Martin Kämpchen, dated 30 April 1989.
58. Amal Home, '*Rabindranath through Western Eyes: By Dr A Aronson.*

*M.A. (Cantab) with a Preface by Dr Amiya Chakravarty*', in *VBQ*, November 1943-January 1944, pp. 262-8.

59. Ibid., p. 267.
60. Aronson, *Rabindranath through Western Eyes*, p. vii.
61. See Dr Uma Das Gupta's notes.
62. The 'Introduction' is dated July 1942. The manuscript is at RBh.
63. Ibid., p. 1.
64. Letter to Martin Kämpchen, dated 29 January 1995.
65. Alex Aronson, *Romain Rolland: The Story of a Conscience*, Bombay: Padma Publications, 1944.
66. See K[rishna] K[ripalani]'s review in *VBQ*, November 1944-January 1945, pp. 147f. He calls it an 'excellent book' (p. 148) and praises it throughout.
67. Aronson, pp. 147-81.
68. Krishna Kripalani/Alex Aronson, *Rolland and Tagore*, Calcutta: Visva-Bharati, 1945.
69. Alex Aronson, *Europe Looks at India: A Study in Cultural Relations*, Bombay: Hind Kitabs, 1946; republished Romain Rolland, *The Story of a Conscience*, Calcutta: Riddhi-India, 1979.
70. Letter to Martin Kämpchen, dated 29 January 1995.
71. Aronson's German passport had expired.
72. *VBN*, October 1939, p. 31.
73. Aronson, *Brief Chronicles of the Time*, p. 73.
74. From 3 September 1939 until 7 November 1939. See Rabindranath Tagore's letter to Sir Reginald Maxwell, dated 4 August 1940 (Alex Aronson's archive).
75. See letter to Martin Kämpchen, dated 29 January 1995.
76. See note 74.
77. Alex Aronson's archive.
78. Rabindranath Tagore's letter, dated 4 September 1940, was reproduced in a Bangladeshi weekly on 29 October 1993. The name of the weekly could not be ascertained.
79. Letter to Martin Kämpchen, dated 29 January 1995.
80. Letter dated 20 November 1939 (Alex Aronson's archive).
81. Aronson, *Brief Chronicles of the Time*, p. 112.
82. Aronson, *For the Time Being*, p. 35.
83. See Martin Kämpchen, 'A Friend of India', in *The Statesman*, Calcutta/ Delhi, 15 October 1994 (Literary Supplement).
84. Alex Aronson, *Selected Poems*, Calcutta: Writers Workshop, 1989, pp. 19-30.
85. See letter to Martin Kämpchen, dated 20 April 1993.
86. Aronson, *Brief Chronicles of the Time*, p. 5.
87. Letter to Martin Kämpchen, dated 9 February 1995.

9. Alex Aronson in his study
at Santiniketan, 1940.

10. Rabindranath Tagore at Santiniketan on the occasion of the award of an honorary doctorate from the University of Oxford in 1940.

11. Alex Aronson receiving his honorary doctorate from Visva-Bharati University of Santiniketan through the hands of Martin Kämpchen as delegate of the University in 1993 in Haifa, Israel.

VISVA-BHARATI

FOUNDER-PRESIDENT
RABINDRANATH TAGORE

SANTINIKETAN
BENGAL, INDIA.

September 4, 1940

Dear Sir Nazimuddin,

I am enclosing herewith copy of a letter I recently wrote to the Home Member to the Government of India and his reply to it. Soon after the commencement of the war, Dr. Aronson was taken into a concentration camp. The Principal of our College, the department to which he belongs, saw you in person on our behalf. I also wrote to you asking for special consideration. I have reasons to believe your intercession in his behalf secured his early release. He may be taken away once again to a 'parole settlement'; by orders of the Government he should be ready to go by September 30 I understand the Government is now examining the details of each individual case. It will be a very great favour shown to the Visva-Bharati if you will put in a word in his favour.

He volunteered his services for war purposes on three occasions since the outbreak of war. His need here is very great, as he is specially in charge of the examinees. I cannot easily replace him and our educational work will considerably suffer if he is removed from our midst. If in the opinion of the Government he can be safely allowed to remain in freedom, will you kindly also secure his exemption from war voluntary work for which he has offered his services.

I know you are very busy and I will ask you not to trouble yourself to reply. I have to make my representation however as President of the Visva-Bharati.

With kind regards, Yours sincerely,

The Hon'ble Khwaja Sir Nazimuddin, K.C.I.E.

Rabindranath Tagore

12. Letter of Rabindranath Tagore to Khwaja Sir Nazimuddin, Santiniketan, 4 Sept. 1940

# Under the Spell of the Mahatma: Dr Margarete Spiegel

*Johannes H. Voigt*

> He was sitting in the court of the jail under a Mango-tree, surrounded by a group of women and men. I was thinking of Jesus or Socrates. This first meeting of him was the most impressive experience I have ever had in my life. I felt the magic fascination, which emanates from a truly great man. He, the prisoner, was the real master, the jail warder bowing towards him in reverence.
>
> (Translated from Dr Margarete Spiegel, 'Erinnerungen an Mahatma Gandhi', in *Deutsch-indische Blätter*, Bombay: July 1968

These words were part of Margarete Spiegel's reminiscences of Mahatma Gandhi, written shortly before her death on 13 June 1968 in Bombay. From her first meeting with Gandhi in October or November 1932, which her words relate to, she remained for the rest of her life under the spell of the Mahatma, whom she venerated as a god-like person. Inspired by his principles, she led an unostentatious life, shunning all publicity, hardly being recognized by her contemporaries.

## MARGARETE SPIEGEL AND HER LIFE IN GERMANY

Who was Margarete Spiegel? Although quite a number of letters written by Gandhi to her have been preserved and published in his *Collected Works*, very little is known about her. It was not easy to unravel facts about her German background, as she left Germany for good in 1933, either taking her personal notes and letters with her to India or leaving them in Berlin with her mother. Some official documents and a few unpublished letters to Gandhi was all the source material available to put some features of her character and experiences together, giving clues of her attachment to the Mahatma and India.

Margarete Spiegel was born on 11 October 1897 in Berlin as the only daughter of Joseph Spiegel, a merchant, and his wife Franziska, née Abraham.[1] In her brief reminiscences she confesses that she had been interested in India ever since her childhood, having been attracted to Indian religions and the principle of *ahimsa* (non-violence) with Gandhi as its prophet.[2] If that was the case—and we have no reason to doubt it—we may well assume that her inclinations were a reaction to the militaristic spirit which pervaded Germany and Berlin, in the centre of which she was living, and also a reaction to the First World War, which broke out when she was 17 years old.

Margarete attended ten forms of the Dorotheenlyzeum and then the Humanistische Studienanstalt of the Augustaschule in Berlin, where she passed her *Abitur*, i.e. her final school examination at Easter in 1918. She studied for eight semesters philology in a number of subjects: English, Romance and Indo-Germanic languages at the universities of Erlangen, Berlin, Munich and Bonn. Her doctoral dissertation, accepted at Bonn University in 1921, was on *Völkernamen als Epitheta im Gallo-Romanischen* (Names of nations as epithets in Gallo-Romance languages).[3]

The choice of this subject is indicative of her philosophical and political inclinations, viz., to look for epithets in languages given to foreign nations. Margarete Spiegel found out that the number of bad qualities attributed to foreign nations surpassed that of good qualities. This confirmed her suspicion and served her as a warning not to trust and rely on epithets as these were generally born out of prejudices.

For her state examination in 1922, Margarete wrote an essay on the subject *Die pädagogischen Leitgedanken der Landerziehungsheime* (The leading educative principles of the country boarding schools).[4] What may be concluded from that? The choice of this topic meant that she was searching for alternatives in the field of education and hoping to find them in those boarding schools established by Hermann Lietz before the First World War, in the countryside, far away from crowded cities, with teaching in a community life and closer to the resources of nature. In her *curriculum vitae* of 23 January 1922 she confessed that her ideal was to devote her life to teaching and join a *Landerziehungsheim*.[5] Despite basic differences there are similarities between the *Landerziehungsheime* far from the milling crowds in the cities and Gandhi's ashrams in India.

Margarete Spiegel was, for unknown reasons, not able to follow her ideals in Germany, getting her teacher's training and her early teaching positions only in the city of Berlin and its environs. In 1929 she attained a permanent post as *Studienrätin* at the Richard Wagner Oberlyzeum at Friedrichshagen on the eastern fringe of Berlin, teaching English, French, Italian and comparative philology.[6] In her English lessons of an advanced level (in 1932), she chose as a reading text for her pupils *Mahatma Gandhi—Selections from His Writings* (edited by Jutta Tiedemann).[7] Margarete Spiegel's choice of the text was certainly not coincidental at a time when the Weimar Republic was shaken by political crises with increasing violence in the streets and rumours in the air that Hitler and his National Socialists might soon come to power.

In October 1932, Margarete Spiegel took unpaid leave for three months to travel to India and visit Gandhi, in order to see for herself the Mahatma and the way of life in the ashram and understand his ideals and problems.[8] No doubt, there had been other Germans or German-speaking people paying a passing visit to Gandhi, but usually with journalistic intentions or a tourist's inquisitiveness, resulting in hotch-potch semi-sensational publications such as by Franziska Standenath, *Vier Monate zu Gast Mahatma Gandhis. Indiens Freiheitskampf 1930. Gefängnisbriefe des Mahatma aus der Zeit vom 31.Juli bis 6.November 1930* (Graz, Wien, Leipzig 1930). Such products were merely scratching the surface of Gandhi's life and ideals. Margarete Spiegel was searching for more, as her expectations reveal and, indeed, led to the greatest experience of her life.

On her return to Germany, she became witness to her home country in the grip of National-Socialism when Hitler was appointed chancellor on 30 January 1933. The new anti-Semitic atmosphere was immediately apparent. She felt ostracized and wrote to Gandhi: 'At present more than ever I feel what the Harijans feel—as a Jewess. One teacher keeps calling me an Asiatic (the complete term is an "Asiatic subman"), [a literal translation of '*asiatischer Untermensch*'—author] of course, I am honoured by that name, because you are an Asiatic too.'[9]

It was during those weeks of dramatic change in Germany that Margarete Spiegel along with her schoolgirls of an advanced class was reading Mahatma Gandhi's texts from *Young India* (1919-22). The educational effect, however, was disappointing; in her words 'miserable', as she reported to Gandhi: 'Out of 20 girls I have not converted a single one to ahimsa. Am I such a bad teacher? Does my enthusiasm provoke a reaction on the girls?' Trying to explain her 'failure' she attributed it to a climate pervaded with violence:' 'They (i.e. the girls) have only four lessons [per week—author] with me and thirty with others all of whom reveal violence. Fancy, when I was reading my favourite passage—about the cow—to them, they burst out laughing, so I stopped because that was sacrilege.'[10]

Gandhi tried to console her:

You need not worry over the poor comprehension that your girls have shown to ahimsa. I do not wonder. There is no response to ahimsa from the atmosphere. They have never been taught to attach the slightest value to it, and probably they have been taught to despise it. You cannot expect them all of a sudden to understand the value of ahimsa in an atmosphere so hostile as yours.[11]

The Mahatma was right: the atmosphere in Germany was one of violence, but he probably did not realize that the girls in Margarete's class certainly knew her to be a Jewess and took the Gandhi reader most probably as a sign of personal defence.

Threatened by the infamous law for the restoration of the German professional civil service of early April 1933, Margarete Spiegel left Germany for India forthwith, using her still valid visa. According to her personal file from the school administration and according to a report of her school, she was dismissed from service on 1 October 1933 by an order of 26 September based on the aforementioned notorious Law.[12]

Her colleagues as well as the teaching profession in Germany may have been surprised to find an article by her on the subject 'Mahatma Gandhi und die indische Frau (Eindrücke von einer Studienreise)' in the professional journal of lady-teachers, the *Deutsche Lehrerinnenzeitung* of 20 July 1933. In this article, published at a time when the Nazis were firmly established in the centres of power, Margarete Spiegel describes, in a first part the Mohammedan purdah system, then customs of child marriage and so on, while in the second she turns to Gandhi's 'discovery' of the Indian women's role in economic, social and political life. She gives a detailed account of the women's role in Gandhi's ashram and in India's political struggle: 'Mahatmaji's struggle is non-violent, he fights only with spiritual weapons. And in this struggle, in which devotion is the essence, a woman is at least a match for a man, if not more than a match. . . . India's fate depends on her women, for in their hands lies the education of their children.'[13]

The concluding paragraph is a confession of her sentiments and a homage to the Mahatma:

No man has ever shown more understanding of women than ascetic Mahatma Gandhi. To him all women are sisters. As he is free from all passions, he is able to discover the soul of a woman as no other man can. He holds the woman's intuition as more important than the superior knowledge of a man. In his eyes, a woman is the embodiment of devotion; therefore, he regards her as nobler than man. The Mahatma calls women 'the better half of humanity, not the weaker sex.[14]

The article by Margarete Spiegel was a kind of legacy to women in the country of her birth. We do not know of any reactions to this writing of hers.

MARGARETE SPIEGEL IN INDIA

Margarete Spiegel arrived in Bombay on 27 April 1933 to stay in India as a refugee. She went straight to Poona (now Pune) to meet Gandhi who was again in prison. Proposing to enter the ashram, she left her valuables at his disposal, as she stated in her testament:

I leave the money and all the things I have got with me to Mahatma Gandhi's Ashram and for the Harijans' cause. The things they do not want are not to be destroyed, they are to be given to other people. In order to save the money for my burial, I leave my dead body for dissection to the Sassoon Hospital in Poona (from Berlin-Friedrichshagen, Rahnsdorfer Str. 34a).[15]

This last will and the accompanying letter to Gandhi has been written on the stationery of the Servants of India Society, Poona. In her reminiscences she makes particular mention of her golden necklace which she handed over to Gandhi in the jail court, who then named her Amala, meaning 'without impurity'.[16]

The correspondence between Gandhi and Amala, of which, apart from four early writings, only the letters of Gandhi have been preserved, reflect the problems of integration and acclimatization facing the former Jewish high school teacher from Berlin. Gandhi cared so much about the continuation of his correspondence with her after his imprisonment that he asked the Home Secretary of Bombay Government specifically to be allowed to write to an American lady in his fold, Neela Devi, and to Dr Margarete Spiegel, as they were 'comparative strangers to India and otherwise require delicate attention'. Therefore, he 'should like to be able to write to them and

Sjt. Vinoba who is in charge of Wardha Ashram and who is to look after them'.[17] The two persons in his care indicated the spectrum of the Mahatma's humanitarian concerns: the American lady was a so-called 'fallen woman' with a son, and Margarete Spiegel a refugee, persecuted in her home country for racist reasons.

From Sabarmati Ashram, threatened to be taken over by the government, Margarete Spiegel was transferred with some other Europeans to Wardha. In order to make sure that the British-Indian authorities did not lay hands on foreign inmates of the ashram, which could mean for Margarete Spiegel extradition and repatriation to Nazi Germany, Gandhi gave an interview to the *Times of India* assuring that Margarete and two other 'Europeans', viz., Neela Devi and Duncan Greenless, were merely 'qualifying for Harijan service', i.e. not being involved in political activities of the freedom movement.[18]

It was soon apparent, however, that Margarete Spiegel, though prepared to do all that was required of her in the ashram, was ill-suited for manual work. Gandhi kept on asking her about her progress in spinning, once calling the threads she had spun 'ropes'. He admonished her constantly to concentrate on training for Harijan service, as on 1 August 1933: 'You will not be fit for Harijan work if you do not concentrate and learn to use your hands well. Your spinning is most clumsy.'[19] He disliked all intellectual aberrations, even her interest in the *Gita*: 'I wonder what you mean when you say you read the *Gita* every day. . . . Vinoba is quite right in asking you to learn cooking, Hindi and cotton processes well, if you do real work amongst Harijans.'[20] Mirabehn, he thought, spending four hours daily teaching Margarete, was wasting her time![21] Only towards the end of the first year did he discover some progress: 'I see that you are spinning much better than you used to. . . .'

The crowning reward of all her toil was the Mahatma's invitation to accompany him on part of his Harijan tour, from Kanpur to Benares (now Varanasi). They were due to stay for eight days in the holy city on the Ganga, being the guests of Kashi Vidyapith, a nationalist college. After that she left the ashram in November 1934.[22]

Gandhi realized that even though Margarete was ill-suited for manual work needed for Harijan service, she was well prepared for learning and teaching languages, making quick progress in Hindi, Gujarati and Bengali, provoking favourable comments from Gandhi. A few years later, Gandhi, comparing her to Max Mueller, recommended her devotion to language learning as a model: 'Amala knows

13 languages and can even teach some of them. Max Mueller knew 14 languages including Latin, Greek, Hebrew and Sanskrit. He could even correspond in Sanskrit.' Gandhi was modest enough to admit that he had not been devoted to learning foreign languages: 'I am sorry that I was never able to learn German.'[23]

It seemed for a while that Margarete would find a position at Tagore's university at Santiniketan; but for some reason or the other, it did not work out. She eventually settled down in Bombay to earn her living by teaching. Gandhi consoled her about what she regarded a meagre income: 'Be content with what you are getting. Rs. 50 plus Rs. 25 should be enough for you.' And a month later: 'I am glad your income is increasing by leaps and bounds. No wonder you like Bombay.'[24]

Margarete Spiegel felt a strong attachment to the Mahatma, which was difficult for her to control. Gandhi, on the other hand, was rather critical of her, mainly on account of her sentimental approach and, as stated earlier, for her want of practical faculties. Writing to his nephew Narandas Gandhi, in charge of the ashram at Sabarmati, two days after her arrival in Bombay, the Mahatma presented a straightforward assessment of her:

> Margarete is a different type [i.e. different from Neela—author]. She is 35 years old and, therefore, her character is practically formed. She is a woman of great learning and is quick in learning things by heart, but she is not very intelligent. She is obstinate, but her motives are pure. I think her life has been blameless. She has great love for the Ashram. But she has no sense of proportion when she speaks. Ever since she has been here, she has been talking about the Ashram in season and out of season. She has left the country and come to India because of the movement in Germany against her but she has no plan before her.[25]

Occasionally, he was even more frank, e.g. to Mirabehn he once wrote: 'Margarete Spiegel, who is named Amala, is as mad as a mad-hatter. But what was one to do? She simply came and one had to take her.' He did not hide his anger and scorn. Thus he wrote in a letter to Margarete: 'I have your two stupid and silly letters. I never knew that you were so unbalanced, suspicious and hypersensitive.' It seems that Gandhi had to curb the emotional attachment that Margarete Spiegel felt towards him, pulling her back to the realities of life: 'Do become steady. It is not good to be constantly thinking of being with me.' And nine months later in a similar vein: 'Can you not see that it is impossible for all who love me to be physically with me?'[26]

Her attachment to the Mahatma made a natural integration with her new environment very difficult. She toyed with the idea of suicide, but Gandhi tried to dissuade her: 'You ought to be steady and brave. To deserve to die is cowardice. There is nobody about you who has any wish to repress you. You have built in front of you a mountain of difficulties. Make your choice reasonably and act.' He scolded and admonished her again and again to come to terms with realities: 'You must compose yourself and live and think naturally. If you love me, you cannot fear me.'[27]

Gandhi learnt about the racist policy of the Nazis in Germany and the persecution of Jewish Germans in its first phase from Margarete Spiegel, herself a victimized witness. To what extent she was able to provide general information is difficult to make out, as obviously all her later letters have been lost. One source of further information was most probably Margarete Spiegel's mother, who was living in Berlin. In the early years, Margarete fretted at her hasty emigration, leaving her mother alone in the German capital. Gandhi advised her to choose one of the alternatives, viz., either to return to Germany or to get herself immersed in Harijan work.[28] As the first course was impossible, there remained only the second choice.

Why Margarete Spiegel asked Gandhi to write to her mother is open to question; the letter does not seem to have been preserved. Maybe its loss explains its purpose: it was written for protecting Franziska Spiegel in Berlin from molestation or persecution and to demonstrate to the authorities that her daughter was, so to speak, in 'good hands', viz., Gandhi's, and by that protection to ward off interrogations about the disappearance of Margarete and harm to herself. For, in those months, from June to September 1933, Margarete was still legally a German civil servant tied by an oath to the German state. It is likely that Gandhi's letter helped her mother to leave Germany three years later and join Margarete in Bombay.

Margarete Spiegel had problems with her identity. She was born a German citizen and retained her citizenship for a few years to come; by denomination she was Jewish, by her attachment to Gandhi she was assumed to be a Hindu. Gandhi tried to dissuade her of the latter: 'You do not need to be a Hindu but a true Jewess. If Judaism does not satisfy you, no other faith will give you satisfaction for any length of time. I would advise you to remain a Jewess and appropriate the good of the other faiths.'[29]

Gandhi, though informed about the Nazi terror in Germany, was unable to fathom its viciousness and violence. In a number of interviews and articles, he had only one answer to give to meet the brutalities of the state: the resort to a non-violent resistance. He believed that the mehods he had used in South Africa and India would have the same effect in Germany, viz., to defeat the stronger forces of the Nazi state morally. After the infamous pogrom of the 'Reichskristallnacht' of 9/10 November 1938, he made known his opinion, that if ever a war—rejecting this though on principle—were to be waged for a justifiable cause, it was a war against Germany because of the persecution of her Jewish citizens.[30] He was keen to learn what Margarete Spiegel thought of his statements.[31] Her reply is not known.

## CONCLUSION

The one and a half years of Margarete Spiegel's stay in Gandhi's ashrams and her exchange of views with him about her own problems and those of her work for the lowest in the community remained the central experience of her life. She had taken roots in India despite great disappointments. She realized, with the help of Gandhi, that she herself was the problem and not her Indian environment or the Mahatma's paternal attitude. She had lost her connections with her country of birth whence she returned after the end of the war for a short stay only.[32]

Mahatma Gandhi remained a spiritual fountain for her during the 20 years she was to survive him. Declining to write her own personal memoirs, she sat down shortly before her death to compose her reminiscences of the Mahatma, who had offered her refuge and given her psychological help and a spiritual hold in a period of darkness for mankind in general and for Jews in particular.

## NOTES

1 Zeugnis über die wissenschaftliche Prüfung für das Lehramt an höheren Schulen. Dr. phil. Margarete Spiegel. Bonn: 22 July 1922. Archiv der Rheinischen Friedrich-Wilhelms-Universität, Bonn.

2. Dr Margarete Spiegel, 'Erinnerungen an Mahatma Gandhi', in *Deutsch-indische Blätter. Beilage der Indo-German Review*, Bombay: July 1968, pp. iiif., vi und viii.

3. Margarete Spiegel, Lebenslauf. Bonn: 23 January 1922. Anhang zum Zeugnis (s.footnote 1). Liste der besuchten Vorlesungen in Berlin.

Ibid. Belegbogen der Vorlesungen in München, Sommersemester 1920. Archiv der Ludwig-Maximilians-Universität, Munich. Promotionsdiplom, 24 November 1921. Archiv der Friedrich-Wilhelms-Universität, Bonn; Margarete Spiegel, *Völkernamen als Epitheta im Gallo-Romanischen*. Berlin: 1921.

4. Zeugnis (footnote 1).
5. See note 3.
6. Höhere Lehranstalten. Personalblatt. A. Margarete Spiegel. Berliner Institut für Lehrerfort-und-weiterbildung und Schulentwicklung. Und *Philologen-Jahrbuch für das höhere Schulwesen Preußens und einiger anderer deutscher Länder*. 37.Jg. Breslau 1930, p. 359.
7. Spiegel, 'Erinnerungen', 1968, p. iii.
8. Ibid.
9. Spiegel to Gandhi, 27 February 1933. National Gandhi Museum, New Delhi.
10. Ibid.
11. Gandhi to Spiegel, 24 March 1933, in *The Collected Works of Mahatma Gandhi* (henceforth *CW*), Vol. 54, pp. 180ff.
12. Lucy S. Davidowicz, *Der Krieg gegen die Juden 1933-45*. Wiesbaden: Fourier Verlag, 1979. Und Paul Hilberg, *Die Vernichtung der europäischen Juden*. Frankfurt/M.: Fischer Taschenbuch Verlag, 1994, Vol. 1, pp. 87ff. Spiegel, 'Erinnerungen', 1968, p. iv. Höhere Lehranstalten, Personalblatt A (last entry: '1 Oct. 1933 entlassen B (erufs) B (eamten) G (esetz)'. (Note 6).
13. Dr Margarete Spiegel, 'Mahatma Gandhi und die indische Frau (Eindrücke einer Studienreise)' in *ADLV. Deutsche Lehrerinnenzeitung. Organ des Allgemeinen Deutschen Lehrerinnenvereins i.L.* Berlin: 20 July 1933, pp. 241f.
14. Ibid., p. 242.
15. Spiegel, 'Testament of Dr.Margarete Spiegel', Poona, Servants of India Society, 2 May 1933. National Gandhi Museum, New Delhi.
16. Spiegel, 'Erinnerungen', 1968, p. iv.
17. 6 August 1933. *CW*, Vol. 55, p. 347. Vinoba Bhave was an associate of the Mahatma.
18. 27 August 1933. Ibid., p. 316.
19. 1 August 1933. Ibid., p. 337.
20. 26 August 1933. Ibid., p. 377.
21. 29 September 1933. *CW*, Vol. 56, p. 36. Mirabehn—Gandhi's name for M. Slade, an English lady, who was a close follower of his.
22. Spiegel, 'Erinnerungen', 1968, p. iv.
23. Gandhi to Kantilal Gandhi, 10 January 1938. *CW*, Vol. 66, p. 333. And Gandhi to Spiegel, 5 March 1934. Ibid., Vol. 57, p. 248.
24. 18 October 1935 and 15 November 1935. *CW*, Vol. 62, pp. 40 and 117.

25. 29 April 1933. *CW*, Vol. 55, p. 69.
26. 7, 9 and 22 June 1933 and 29 March 1934. *CW*, Vol. 55, pp. 188, 191 and 216, and Vol. 57, p. 325.
27. 2 and 15 December 1933. *CW*, Vol. 56, pp. 298 and 339.
28. 26 June 1933. *CW*, Vol. 55, p. 217.
29. 15 March 1934. *CW*, Vol. 57, p. 278.
30. Gandhi's articles on the persecution of Jews in Germany in *CW*, Vol. 68, pp. 137-41, 191-3, 276-8 and 381f.
31. 5 December 1938, *CW*, Vol. 68, p. 183.
32. Ernest N. Shaffer, *Ein Emigrant entdeckt Indien*, München: Verlag Information und Wissen, 1971, pp. 159f.

# RECEPTIONS AND REFLECTIONS

# Interculturality: A View from Below
# Anita Desai's *Baumgartner's Bombay*

*Rainer Lotz and Rekha Kamath*

The theme of Central European emigration to India between 1933 and 1945 opens up avenues of historical and sociological inquiry that have not been explored systematically till now. Prior to scholarly interest in the subject creative writers have taken up the theme as the focus or the framework of their novels. One prominent example is Anita Desai's novel *Baumgartner's Bombay*,[1] a story centred around the life ot a German Jewish emigrant to India.[2] The novel narrates the story of Baumgartner's life and depicts the existential aspect of a condition of exile and migration. Our analysis of the novel will, therefore, attempt to view this theme through the prism of literary aesthetics and seek to understand its connotations for creative writing.

Let us keep in mind the specific qualities of the object we are looking at. Like academic studies this novel too draws on historical sources. Yet it is a statement on contemporary times meant for a contemporary audience. In view of the recent debates on the rhetorics of historiography, the distinction between a literary text and that of a historian might not be sustainable any longer. What we are going to discuss, however, is a work of fiction which takes the scattered evidence found after the death of an Austrian Jew in Bombay[3] as a starting point for a narrative which covers almost the whole lifetime of the protagonist: from his early childhood days in Berlin to his sudden death presumably in the 1980s. Being a work of fiction, this text cannot be equated with historiography in the way sources are treated and processed in the novel. The text's significance for us does not rest on the presentation of a verifiable account of events, persons, dates and places. As our analysis will show, the perspectives of the novel are not centred primarily on the study of Indian Jewish identity.[4] They connote rather the history of a Jewish emigrant's exile in India with the issue of 'translation' and reinterpretation of a person's identity in an age of migration. Against this background it allows a reading in the context of issues raised in recent years by several authors and critics of Indian writing in English literature.[5] This perspective culminates in the issue of how to conceive of, or even establish, a cultural identity in the concerned individuals and groups.

The protagonist of the novel, Hugo Baumgartner, first appears as a decrepit old man, unwashed and unkempt, who has lived in India for the last 50 years. Living in a state of penury, he occupies a flat in a ramshackle old building in Bombay with only his stray cats for company. Alternating between the narrative past and the present, the novel captures Baumgartner's lonely childhood and youth in Berlin, where he experiences early on what it meant to be different from the world and the people around him. The events unfolding in Fascist Germany thrust his Jewishness upon him and force him to leave the country. He comes to India—not as a matter of choice, but because of business links in the timber trade with his father's erstwhile firm. The novel then highlights different episodes in Baumgartner's life during the pre-war period in Calcutta, the years of internment as an enemy alien during the war and lastly the period of employment in Bombay with his friend Chimanlal, after whose death Baumgartner retreats into a near-total isolation:

> He felt his life blur, turn grey, like a curtain wrapping him in its dusty felt. If he became aware, from time to time, that the world beyond the curtain was growing steadily more crowded, more clamorous, and the lives of others more hectic, more chaotic, then he felt only relief that his had never been part of the mainstream. Always, somehow, he had escaped the mainstream. (p. 211)

It is this marginality which characterizes Baumgartner's life and personality. Marginality can occur as a result of emigration, as a necessary correlate to being cut off from one's own national, racial and linguistic identity. These usual connotations of exile and emigration as a literary theme are relegated to the background here, since Baumgartner's isolation from the mainstream cannot be explained wholly in these terms. On the one hand, there is practically nothing which connects him with Germany after the death of his mother, and, on the other hand, he feels no sentimental attachment to the German language either, which he feels 'slipping away from him' (p. 150). He is, in fact, characterized by a complete absence of any self-defined identity, since he does not project himself either in terms of being a German, a Jew or even a naturalized Indian. Rather, his person functions as an 'empty space' onto which others project their constructed versions of his identity, which Baumgartner accepts stoically along with the consequences that such identities entail. In Germany he was marked 'the Jew', in British India the 'enemy alien', and in independent India he was the '*firanghi*', the foreigner. In different situations Baumgartner becomes the victim of different identities that are thrust on him.

> Accepting—but not accepted; that was the story of his life, the one thread that ran through it all. In Germany he had been dark—his darkness had marked him the Jew, der Jude. In India he was fair—and that marked him the firanghi, the foreigner. In both lands, the unacceptable. (p. 20)

This process of ascribing of an identity continues till the end, when Baumgartner is asked by the Parsi café owner Farrokh to look after a young German hippie. The chain of events thus set in motion and which end with Baumgartner's brutal murder by the young drug addict have their origin in Baumgartner being identified as a German by Farrokh. Baumgartner's death too, is therefore, a consequence of an identity which is ascribed to him by others. However secluded a life one may lead—and Baumgartner is an extreme example of this self-contained seclusion—it seems impossible to escape the boundaries of a national, a racial or a linguistic identity. Baumgartner's tragedy evolves precisely around such dividing distinctions. Seen from the perspective of Farrokh, the young hippie and Baumgartner are connected qua origin despite the differences in age and lifestyle. It is a commonality of a 'they' versus an 'us'. This assumption disturbs the monotonous placidity of Baumgartner's daily routine, and he finds himself not only thinking of his past, but also reflecting on his distance to the country he has lived in for 50 years. Long suppressed memories resurface; memories that he must face up to, perhaps for the first time in all these years:

> What did the boy mean to him with his filthy yellow curls and his ridiculous silver bracelet? There was no reason why he should be stirred by his fairness or his filth, or his misfortune. . . . Well, he knew. He might try to hurry away and rid himself of the fact but it was there: the boy was German, was he not? Yes, that was it. A German from Germany. He had sensed, he had smelt the German in him like a cat might smell another and know its history, its territory. (p. 21)

On the one hand, it could be argued that Baumgartner's own attitudes notwithstanding, there is more to his identity as a German than he himself would like to admit after all these years of staying in India. On the other hand, it becomes apparent that the national identity is linked up in Baumgartner's mind with the problem of being a German Jew, for the young hippie reminds Baumgartner of a 'certain type that [he] had escaped, forgotten' (p. 21). Yet when Baumgartner takes the boy home with him, he is unable to explain to himself the reasons behind this act. One could interpret the act as yet another example of Baumgartner's stoic acceptance of the various identities thrust upon him, whereby he remains a victim of the consequences. The possibility of this interpretation is undermined to some extent, however, when Baumgartner himself ascribes his impulsive act to the dictates of 'blood': 'Why? Baumgartner, Baumgartner, he sighed, ask your blood why it is so, only the blood knows' (p. 152).

This could perhaps imply, as mentioned earlier, that despite his feeling of not belonging anywhere, in the depths of his consciousness, a spark of his German heritage is still alive. This view is underscored by the German nursery rhymes that are frequently interspersed in the text and which evoke an unconscious 'sense of belonging'. Ironically, it is this heritage which leads to his death—an end he thought he had escaped by emigration. In the end it is the blood that answers—the blood spattered all over the room in which Baumgartner is murdered in a manner as clumsy as it is gruesome .

Baumgartner's exile in Bombay is not the fate of the uprooted exile who returns home when conditions become more favourable, moves on elsewhere or settles down in the land of his exile by choice. India, the country where Baumgartner has spent 50 years of his life, is not a country where he has consciously chosen to stay on. His remaining there has merely 'happened' to him, like everything else in his life. In a conversation with his only friend Lotte, who shares a similar fate, the absence of choice becomes very apparent:

> Everyone was like that in the war. . . . People made money, made fortunes—then vanished. . . . Only we stayed, like fools. . . . Where could we go, Lotte? Where could you and I have gone? . . . Yes, there was nowhere to go. Germany was gone—phut. Europe was gone, all of it. Let us face it, *Liebchen*, there is no home for us. (pp. 80f.)

What is described here is the condition of the existentially homeless, the eternally exiled, the existential outsiders who belong nowhere.[6] Although the 'entire world is a foreign land to him', Baumgartner is not made to appear as the 'perfect man',[7] the champion of multiculturality, the cosmopolitan outsider by choice. He is not a sovereign member of various societies, let alone of a global culture, but an individual driven and battered by circumstances. Neither is Baumgartner the post-colonial subject, who is constantly aware of the fragmentation of identities. In the figure of Baumgartner, Anita Desai has created the counterpart to the post-modern cosmopolitan who celebrates his 'borderness'.[8] What characterizes Baumgartner is his marked indifference to all assertions of cultural identities and origins, his own included.

Baumgartner's energy goes into making a living, carving out some niche for himself in order that he may survive. Even in the prison camp, where he is interned with Germans who believe in the Nazi regime and its anti-Semitism, he refrains from defining himself or others. This radically pragmatic attitude also marks the way he enters India and starts life here without any fuss. He comes without any preconceived notions of India or the Indians. This indifference to matters of cultural identity, paired with a patient, receptive and pragmatic approach is best depicted in the way Baumgartner perceives his linguistic situation:

He found he had to build a new language to suit these new conditions—German no longer sufficed, and English was elusive. Languages sprouted around him like tropical foliage and he picked words from it without knowing if they were English or Hindi or Bengali—they were simply words he needed: *chai, khana, baraf, lao, jaldi, joota, chota peg, pani, kamra, soda, garee* ... what was this language he was wrestling out of the air, wrenching around to his own purposes? He suspected it was not Indian, but India's, the India he was marking out for himself'. (p. 92)

This passage illuminates a number of points that are worth mentioning: for instance, the situation of the 'insignificant' immigrant, who has to deal with life in a foreign country and adapts to its realities in a way best suited for his own existence. He pragmatically assimilates whatever is required without a thought to its origins or its 'deeper' cultural meaning. *Baumgartner's Bombay* shows the ground realities of a migrant's situation as opposed to debates on 'cultural carelessness and lack of commitment to one's own culture' as we find it, for example, in Jaidev's critique of 'culture of pastiche'.[9] Discussing Hindi novels Jaidev draws an 'important cultural moral': 'Unless we possess a viable, culture-specific identity of our own, we lack substantiality. Without such an identity, we cannot engage in an honourable dialogue with another culture, no matter how devoted we may be to it. We float across cultures, but collect only surface bubbles, their clichés.

Light things float.'[10] This reads well as long as we view it in the context of a struggle against the hegemony of 'Western culture: in a post-colonial society'.[11] However, such a catalogue is only conceived of, or takes place, in an élite culture of intellectuals and artists. In view of the 'overall realities', Jaidev and Aijaz Ahmad demand it,[12] but we find that in everyday life there is hardly any space for a dialogue which would be free from inequalities and projections. On the surface Anita Desai's novel could be seen as proving the point that by his indifference and lack of commitment the protagonist disqualifies himself as a member of any society. Yet there is more to it when we see that Baumgartner's openness is thwarted by the drive of his various social and cultural environments to put forth exactly what Jaidev and others expect from a modern Indian writer: self-definition and commitment to one's own culture. By stressing these prerequisites there appears to be neither scope for dialogue nor any way to come to terms with issues of ethnicity in a modern urban context. In *Baumgartner's Bombay* two histories confront each other and neither seem to understand or even be interested in one another. Baumgartner, the migrant from Germany, remains to the end external to life in India, just as no one he comes in contact with in the country of his exile understands his history as a German Jew.

Baumgartner almost seems to be modelled according to the features of the migrant Salman Rushdie depicts in *Shame*.[13] Baumgartner too has 'floated up from history, from memory, from Time' (*Shame*, p. 87). In calling Baumgartner a 'translated man' (*Shame*, p. 29) one has to add that no distinct cultural 'original' of his exists either. He is a 'floater' *par excellence*, never quite at home anywhere, 'wrestling out of the air' not only a language, but also a personality and life-style. He is 'not Indian, but India's' inhabitant, much like his friend Lotte, who is not so much his friend because she is German, but because she 'belonged to the India of his own experience' (p. 150). It is the experience of the defeated, the experience of being solitary foreigners each with his or her own history of failure. It would be all too easy to derogatively qualify Baumgartner as a 'vagrant'. He misses out at the very point on which Aijaz Ahmad comes down heavily on Rushdie as a writer: he does not take up a position.[14]

Yet seeing and understanding how throughout his life, Baumgartner falls prey to the ascriptions and definitions forced on him by others proves the idealistic nature of the statement made by Todorov-Said-Auerbach. Positionality is not a question of subjective choice, but a result of definitions of insider and outsider, of us and them, that are voiced and enforced by the environment.

The novel *Baumgartner's Bombay,* therefore, does not treat the theme of exile and emigration with all its attendant connotations of a loss of identity and language as a historical phenomenon only. The literary portrayal of an existential marginality opens up the theme to include its wider implications and makes a statement on migration as a modern condition. The protagonist, however, is not depicted as indulging in an excess of belonging to various cultures, as the post-modernist in Aijaz Ahmad's view supposedly does.[15] Neither are there any signs to support the conclusion that Baumgartner suffers under the experience of fragmentation and not belonging. Baumgartner's story does not overcome the distinctions between different cultural identities, but can be said to undermine them by being ignorant of their applicability. The text provides no outline for a solution, but rather the projection of a cultural utopia. On his way to India Baumgartner spends one week in Venice. During his long and solitary exploration of the city he is suddenly struck by a vision:

> Venice was the East, and yet it was Europe too; it was that magic boundary where the two met and blended, and for those seven days Hugo had been a part of their union. He realised it only now: that during his constant wandering, his ceaseless walking, he had been drawing closer and closer to this discovery of that bewitched point where they became one land of which he felt himself the natural citizen. (p. 63)

It is the perceived simultaneity of East and West, of Asia and Europe, meeting in Venice which generates the feeling that an existential outsider in both Europe and Asia could belong in such a place as Venice, where boundary markings are diffused, where definitions of identity with its attendant inclusions and exclusions are not bogged down by essentialisms. Such essentialisms convey the notion of a centre, which necessarily implies a periphery consisting of all that is perceived of as not belonging to that centre. Emigration is the experience of belonging to a periphery. The rejection of the centre-periphery model, which is portrayed in Baumgartner's experience of Venice, removes the experience of marginalization for a brief moment in his life. Venice is, however, a 'no-man's land', a short interlude which does not play a major role even in Baumgartner's consciousness. The centre-periphery issue does not affect him as he lives his life in the various circumstances that confront him.

## NOTES

1. Anita Desai, *Baumgartner's Bombay*, London: Heinemann, 1988. In the following, the page numbers in brackets after quotations refer to this edition.
2. The Marathi novel *Ranangan* by Vishram Bedekar (1939), also discussed in this volume, is another example.
3. Anita Desai remembers an Austrian Jew in Bombay, who 'used to walk around in the back streets looking for scraps to feed his cats'. After he died, a friend of Desai's who also knew him, handed her a bunch of letters in German left by the old man. She found nothing unusual in the letters except the stamp number on each of them. The letters came from Nazi Germany and were the muted testimony of the Nazi concentration camps. The blank spaces in the letters told a story of their own. And 'because they had been so empty, they teased my mind; I had to supply the missing history to them'. Cf. Suresh C. Saxena, Anita 'Desai's Search for Roots in *Baumgartner's Bombay*', in R.K.Dhawan (ed.), *Indian Women Novelists.* Set I, Vol. iv. New Delhi: Prestige, 1991, p. 140.
4. Cf. Nathan Katz (ed.), *Studies of Indian Jewish Identity*, Delhi: Manohar, 1995.
5. Cf. Viney Kirpal (ed.), *The New Indian Novel in English: A Study of the 1980s*, New Delhi: Allied Publishers, 1990; Emmanuel S. Nelson (ed.), *Reworlding: The Literature of the Indian Diaspora,* New York: Greenword Press; Aijaz Ahmed, *In Theory: Classes, Nations, Literatures,* New Delhi: Oxford University Press, 1994. See also 'Samia Mehrez: Translations and the Post-Colonial Experience: The Francophone North African Text', in Lawrence Venuti (ed.), *Rethinking Translation: Discourse, Subjectivity, Ideology,* London and New York: Routledge, 1992, pp.120-38.
6. This situation is described to some extent in Usha Bande, 'The Outsider Situation in *Baumgartner's Bombay*', in R.K. Dhawan, op. cit., pp. 122-9.
7. This celebratory view of cosmopolitanism refers to a famous quotation from Hugo of St. Victor used by Todorov in *The Conquest of America* (1984), who takes it from Edward Said, who in turn takes it from Erich Auerbach. The full quotation runs thus: 'The man who finds his homeland sweet is still a tender beginner; he to whom every soil is as his native one is already strong; but he is perfect to whom the entire world is as a foreign land.' In Edward Said, *Orientalism*, New York 1985 (1st pub. 1978), p. 259.
8. The term is taken from the essay 'Documented/Undocumented' by the Mexican artist Guillermo Gomez-Pena. 'I live smack in the fissure between two worlds. In my fractured reality there cohabit two histories,

languages, cosmologies, artistic traditions and political systems. . . . My identity now possesses multiple repertories. . . . As a result of this process I have become a cultural topographer, border-crosser and hunter of myths. [Border artists like me] practise the epistemology of multiplicity and a border semiotics. We share thematic interests, like the continual clash with cultural otherness, the crisis of identity, or better said, access to trans- or multi-culturalism, and the destruction of borders therefrom. . . .' in Rick Simonson and Scott Walker (eds.), *The Graywolf Annual Fire: Multicultural Literacy*, Saint Paul: Graywolf Press, 1988, pp. 127-30.

9. Jaidev, *The Culture of Pastiche: Existential Aestheticism in the Contemporary Hindi Novel*, Shimla: Indian Institute of Advanced Studies, 1993, p. 225.
10. Ibid., pp. 225f.
11. Ibid., p. 225.
12. Cf. Ibid., p. 227; Aijaz Ahmad, op. cit., pp. 139, 154f., 157.
13. Salman Rushdie, *Shame*, London: Picador, 1984 (1st pub. 1983).
14. Aijaz Ahmad, op. cit., p. 157.
15. For these distinctions and their relevance in the context of post-colonial literature and societies, cf. Aijaz Ahmad, 'Salman Rushdie's *Shame*', in Aijaz Ahmad, op. cit., pp. 123-58, especially pp. 128-30.

# *Ranangan* or Response in Marathi Literature to the Theme of Jewish Emigration

*Rajendra Dengle*

I am a camera with its shutter open, quite passive, recording, not thinking.

Christopher Isherwood, *A Berlin Diary*

*Ranangan* is a 118-page long narrative by Vishram Bedekar written and published in the year 1939. This is the only prose writing of this author who has otherwise penned four plays, an autobiography and several scripts for the Marathi cinema. When one reads the critical writing in Marathi about *Ranangan* one realizes clearly that this little novella had taken the Marathi literary scene by storm—not so much because of its treatment of the problematics of Jewish emigration but because of its then 'unknown' style, structure and technique of narration and a radically 'foreign' world of experience. It succeeded in projecting itself on the mental screen of the reader. Here are some important reactions to *Ranangan*: 'It is a great, intense, and intensely humane document';[1] 'a devastated fairy tale';[2] 'a work of art that transcends its time—definitely a canonical text';[3] 'a complete and natural novel';[4] 'a turning point in the history of Marathi novel'.[5] They are sincere responses of critics who have the ability to finely open up the structure of the text, work out the specificity of its aesthetics and also the decency to admit that *Ranangan* is an elusive text. The charm of the novella is such that one reads it again and again, never really coming close to the feeling that one has 'fully and completely' understood it. *Ranangan* is a multi-layered text which, when read philosophically, historically and in the tradition of literary hermeneutics, offers a response to Jewish emigration and goes beyond it. The purpose of this exercise is to examine its transcultural, human, secular, anti-Fascist and nuanced nationalist implications.

At this stage it is necessary to get to know the text. And this is where our difficulty begins for, as Vasant Tambe points out, it is impossible to 'tell the story' of *Ranangan*. It has to be read in order to get anywhere near its story.[6] It is not possible, at the same time, to present a close reading of the entire text here. We shall, however, have to read closely three or four sub-texts for they reveal the fluid state of consciousness of the main characters and the speed with which it keeps changing.

This is the story of Chakradhar Widhwans and Herta Van. Chakradhar is alternately the first person narrator and the third person in the narrative. He is a young Maharashtrian man returning home from Europe because of the looming threat of the Second World War. Herta is a young German woman, a Jew, banished from Germany. She is in search of a new home also with her old mother. She is on her way to Shanghai, like many other homeless Jews on an Italian ship. Chakradhar and some other Indians of different religious beliefs, castes are also there completing the polymorphic and polychromatic scene on the ship.[7] The stage is set for the dramatic—or perhaps cinematic presentation of 'a great, intense, and intensely humane document'.[8]

The first chapter—'segment' might be a more apt word—is a first-person narrative which appears to be terribly anxious to win the reader's attention over. It promises him a very novel and exciting 'package'—experience complete with a trip to Europe, along with emotional, physical pleasures and sorrows, the life on board an ocean liner, 'foreign' milieu legitimizing 'authentic' descriptions of tobacco and alcohol consumption, prostitution, erotic relationship with a white woman, bathtub, piano, and dancing—no wonder the Marathi reader of that period lapped it all up. The novella seemed to promise everything in his own language, allowing him to let his fantasy run wild, which a Hindi film was going to do pretty soon, with its heroes in tuxedos playing the piano to a heart-rending song set to Hindustani classical music! But this is one way of looking at it. In today's context it is certainly possible to examine in what other way *Ranangan* can funtion.

Its pace is tremendous. Quick, objective, impressionistic descriptions of the atmosphere at the harbour. Then of the sea. Then of the narrator's own inner state of mind. So quick that it becomes difficult to distinguish between these objects of description. Then comes a statement: 'My journey had ended.'[9] Then the sheer paradoxical sorrow of having come home. At the same time, his own wonderment at this mood: 'My whole world was transformed. It had capsized' (p. 8). Then the beginning of a flashback. Herta's tears. The writer ponders: 'Are words of any use? Could this writing have any purpose? I won't see Herta again. At the peak of youth. The whole world before them. Full of energy. Two human beings come together, hold hands and say, "This is it. We won't meet again." Does this happen in reality? Except for when one is close to death? But it happened like that in our case' (p. 9).

Shift to a hotel room in Bombay. Chakradhar's mental landscape. Again very brisk pace. Memories of London, Paris. Then Berlin, where he has never been. And then the news of Herta's suicide. Herta comes from Berlin. Purpose of writing: Therapy.[10]

> I am trying to write this so that the burden of this sorrow may become a bit lighter. But how to write? Where is the beginning? Where is the end? I feel I am already saying what chronologically ought to be told later. But my world for the time being is all upside down. Beginning, end, the order of the directions—everything seems to have become topsy-turvy. I think I will quieten down a little and then tell you.

In the second segment the narrator of the first becomes the champagne-drinking globe-trotter dandy Chakradhar, Hindu, hedonist, arrogant and yet at the core 'human' in the sense that he is keen to become conscious of, and to develop his, historical horizon. He wants to find out—what he does not know. There is the war looming large on the horizon. Characters like Latif are busy making money out of the war industry and the so-called 'white slave traffic'. Values have become fluid. Love has become a commodity. Everyone seems to be in a hurry to 'enjoy' life to its fullest. The general mood is heady. Chakradhar finds himself on a constant 'high'. There is a background to why he has come to Europe and has been living it up with a vengeance. It is the story of one Uma—his first love—who has left him for another man. He is vain and melancholic at the same time when he tells us that in the two years in Europe he had succeeded in remaining detached while enjoying all kinds of pleasures: 'Now nothing fascinates me. I can not laugh wholeheartedly nor can I cry. It is as if the lake of my emotions has frozen because of the cold European weather. It has turned into ice!' (pp. 32f.).

This is the background against which he meets a British prostitute in Paris. Chakradhar's driver tries to drive her away for she is old: 'Come on, get lost! Boss wants the love of a young, beautiful girl!' She laughs loudly and says: 'You fool! Today or tomorrow there is going to be war! Who knows? May be in two months you will be dead! You imagine love is at all possible in such times? Love is possible when life is stable. Not on a battlefield' (p. 15).

Or, later, when the two of them are inside the hotel room and he asks her how long she can stay, she answers: 'For a prostitute a night means the life of one whole birth. Let the life of this birth be dedicated to you!'[16]

Chakradhar finds these 'barock' kind of responses fascinating for they, while describing the general unstable human situation, in a sense also describe his own present uncertain state of mind, although he does not admit it in so many words. He makes her tell her life story which begins with the outbreak of the First World War when she was sixteen and made to join a 'consignment' of young girls meant for the British soldiers. At the time she thought that she was doing a great service to her country. After the war she is left with no option but to do the only job she knows how to do; but prostitution is illegal in England and that is why she is in Paris. Although there is no further significant reference to this short story narrated 'prestissimo' (Kundera, p. 88), it makes a significant contribution to the development of the main story in the sense that it helps Chakradhar see things in a perspective. Hatred between peoples, emergence of Fascism, of war, and creation of an apparent sense of order juxtaposed with tales of devastation of individual existences. And Chakradhar, whose world had till then been revolving around his own personal problem, his bitter experience of frustrated love, in fact, takes a position: 'I hate this business of war' (p. 21)!

Going home is, therefore, a happy proposition. Completely exhausted by the night life of Paris, Chakradhar looks forward to a relaxed 11-day voyage back home to Bombay where he intends to get off the ship with a casual and carefree smile on his face (p. 23). The life on the ship, seen through his eyes is lively and not without a promise of sexual adventure: 'Ten days. All pleasures and comforts. Food, drink, dance. Only one thing was missing—a woman. Given that, the journey was a sure success. That is how everyone looked at it' (pp. 26f.). Another character, Madnani, wants Chakradhar to join him on a 'hunt'. But when he explains that the girls sitting in the bar are all Germans—'But that is neither here nor there!'—Chakradhar says: 'Excuse me, I have a grudge against Germans. I don't fall for any of these girls' (p. 27). The very next sentence, however, exposes the vanity of this statement: 'In the following half hour I made friends with a German' (p. 27). This one is Lui, the child of another Jewish refugee called Martha. (The Martha-Lui-Dr Shinde triangle forms the other story line running parallel to the main on which is Chakradhar and Herta and signifying the 'selfless, innocent, asexual' aspect of 'love'. All critics agree on this!)

The author notes that during the voyage: 'The ship was moving on quietly. The Gulf of Genoa. Actually the sea here is usually stormy. But today everything was quiet. No movement, no rocking, everybody was happy (p. 31).

Herta and Chakradhar 'meet' each other against this backdrop reflecting natural harmony. The two become aware of each other's presence in the ship's bar and simply go on staring at each other:

It was difficult to explain the meaning of that look. . . . There was no confusion. No suggestion. It was as if unconscious. Perhaps in the beginning there was only surprise, curiosity. Thereafter pure greed of looking. . . . According to Herta, it was her first look of love. To speak for myself—I was surprised by that look. A little attracted. Otherwise no other feeling had touched me. (p. 32)

The characters then play a card game (bridge). The game of bridge comes to an end in the bar and another character Michael begins to count the points. Yet another character, Sahay, says: 'Let it be. Why put down 5-7 points?' Michael shakes his head and says: 'It is these 5-7 points which add up to make a hundred. And hundred points mean three pennies. Must put down honours.' Chakradhar says loudly: 'Ah Michael! You are worse than a Jew!' (p. 33).

Bang! The harmony of the previous scene explodes suddenly. Herta jumps to her feet, takes Mannan's, yet another character, hand and before disappearing on to the deck she pauses for a moment at the entrance and throws a glance in Chakradhar's direction: 'It was not difficult to decipher the meaning of that look. Disappointment, pain and rage! Suddenly a thought came to the mind. Could this girl be a Jew'? (p. 33).

A meeting with another German Jewish fellow traveller Kaitel, follows almost immediately after this incident making Chakradhar more and more introspective. Kaitel tells him: 'I call myself a German. Germany is my homeland. German is my mother tongue. But Germany refuses to call me her son. I am a Jew. Banished. That is why I am on my way to Shanghai. I have no hope of seeing Germany ever again' (p. 36).

At this point it becomes important to take a close look at what is going on in Chakradhar's mind. In fact, the following longish quote should form the nucleus of the whole text revealing a process of rethinking, confirming that finally Chakradhar is sobering down. It articulates a decisive shift from a blasé to a more serious, contemplative attitude to his immediate historical context:

So, these are Jews? In a flash I had got it. Whites are mixing with blacks. The Italian staff on the ship respects us Hindi people but neglects these people. One German girl is after Madnani. The other one a short while ago is about to fall into Mannan's trap. Lui's mother is looking at Shinde, hopeful of affectionate attention. All this had but only one meaning. So, these are Jews! I had heard both authentic and inauthentic descriptions of their persecution. The Nazis are out to annihilate them. Same hatred is taking root in Italy, Hungary, Poland. I had heard about all this. In Bombay, while going to the Grant Medical I had seen the Jewish colony on the Nagpada side. But one never associated with the word 'Jew' what one normally does. Jew means 'ever greedy for money', 'Shylock', 'lack of humaneness', 'reservoir of vices', 'evil incarnate'—everybody thought of Jews like that. But, in spite of having such a miserable fate, these are a truly great people. They cannot call even a square inch of earth their own any more. But the last World War continued for four years only because of their greed for money. The arsenals for the next World War too have been kept fully stacked only by these very people. And they will explode only because the rich Jews will want to take revenge—I knew it: the England-Russia rift, the possibility of America getting drawn into the war, Muslim Arabs turning sympathetic towards Germany because of the fighting in Palestine—wherever you looked—it was the politics of the Jews which lay at the bottom of everything. (pp. 36ff.)

And at this stage, the process of introspection begins:

No country of their own, no mother tongue, but fortunate to carry the main burden of humanity's progress from Jesus Christ to Einstein. Such is this community of the Jews. I looked closely. A whole country is taking revenge on these people! What was their fault? According to the Nazis the Jews betrayed Germany in the last World War. But what if this philosophy of hatred spread in other countries too? Today's four lakh Muslims—could they tomorrow accept in principle that they have to annihilate crores of Hindus? Are Hindu organizations tomorrow going to let rivers of blood flow with the sole aim to finish off the non-Hindu communities? If the marginal communities, which are today coming in the way of national emancipation, tomorrow lose the protection which the foreign power is giving them today for its own interests, then is anyone going to forgive them their crime?

Is this conflagration of hatred going to continue to spread rapidly along with progress? Revenge of the last War is the annihilation of the Jews. I got confused. Germany's position may be right. But this simple Jew sitting before me—what crime could he have committed? Then why was he being sacrificed? Is the calamity of the individual greater or the need of the nation? Not just today, the Jews have been tortured for centuries together. But today's persecution has a new, specific connotation. Is it going to be repeated in the history of different countries? The Muslims conquered Hindustan and made it their own; the Parsees begged and found refuge here and so made Hindustan their own—if this Nazi philosophy of national hatred took root in history then the progress of humanity. . . . A cold shudder ran through my body. Several thoughts. Incoherent. What makes our country our own? After how many years, inhabitance of how many generations does a land acquire the significance of a motherland? Palestine belonged to the Jews, Hindustan belongs to the Hindus. Will it remain like that tomorrow? And whom did Hindustan belong to before the Aryan colonies reached the South? Mother tongue is whose language? The Jews ruined Germany. Yet they still want to be called German, look upon German as their mother tongue—is this merely clever business strategy? What do they themselves really think? What all has contributed to their mental make-up? (pp. 38ff.)

Chakradhar is going to find answers to these questions later when Herta will narrate her own story. But before we come to that it is interesting to see the immediate effect these reflections have on Chakradhar's behaviour, Herta's response to it and also the context in which a foundation is laid for an intense relationship between the two.

The following morning Chakradhar and Herta are in the dining hall. He is impatiently waiting for his breakfast, whereas the Italian waiter is continuing to ignore him. When Chakradhar shows his annoyance, the waiter comes to him and says: 'Take your seat at that table. This table is for the white people. For Blacks like you there are tables over there.' Chakradhar is furious:

I sprang to my feet. Seized him by his neck. The tray, the teapot and the rest of the crockery rattled loudly. Everyone must have been taken aback. . . . I shook him violently and said, 'You swine, say it again and I will make you lick the floor! Get me my oatmeal here and be quick about it!' Everyone came running. The Jews were confused. . . . Two-four waiters came. Their head apologized, made the other one apologize as well. I sat down and began my breakfast after a short while. Perhaps this might not have surprised [me] had it happened in England. At least they are vain about having been the winners. But Italians are the beggars of Europe! The most inferior as far as the whiteness of their skin is concerned! It was sheer goodwill that they could ply their ships to Hindustan. And they should dare to do something like this! My blood was boiling. Finally, when everyone else on the table had got up and left, I felt better. I looked up. Herta was again staring at me. There was affection in her look. I finished my breakfast. Took out the pipe. Struck match after match. Right over me was the ventilator. Its wind would extinguish them. Apart from that my hand was still trembling. I did not notice it. Finally Herta got up, smiling. She turned the face of the ventilator, and the match was lit. I looked up. There was a fresh cigarette in her lips. I lit it and said, 'Thank you so much' and meant it. On her face was a smile of satisfaction. When I put the match to the pipe, I realized that my hand had stopped trembling. (p. 40)

That night when Chakradhar is standing alone on the deck, aware of the presence of an Anglo-Indian woman and a white man in the far corner, there comes the decisive statement from Herta: 'I have come' (p. 42). What follows a little later is a long scene of ecstatic love making. It is Chakradhar's renaissance.[11] Everything has happened so suddenly that his immediate past with its staleness and barrenness and bitterness falls off him, as it were, as he compares his situation to 'a snake shadding its skin' and becoming young again, full of enthusiasm, optimism and energy. All the rubbish that his consciousness had accumulated over the past two years is simply blown away to bits from his beingness (pp. 46f.).

From Herta's point of view, too, it is the taste of the beginning of a new life. She is suddenly fearless. When Chakradhar cautions her that there are other people on the deck who might 'look', she says:

Why should I be afraid of anybody? When this limitless happiness in life is before me, you want me to lose it by being secretive about it? Never. Let them all come! I'll tell them: I have never been happy. I have suffered hell. Now the few moments of happiness I have I am going to live them to the fullest! I'll ring this bell myself, call everybody and tell them that the two of us have become immensely happy. (p. 49)

The tone of these outbursts is once again strikingly 'baroque'. In fact, one is reminded of Martin Opitz's poem, the first verses of which are: '*Ach Liebste lass uns eilen. Wir haben Zeit: Es schadet das Verweilen uns beiderseit.*'[12]

Port Said. Herta is thrilled, dressed up to go ashore and have the time of her life:

I have become human again. Had forgotten that I was the last four-five years! I used to feel I am inferior to the smallest of the small insects! I put my foot on the ship and could breathe the air of freedom. I could not believe it. Here everyone knows you, greets you, speaks to you, laughs, plays. You spoil me, look after me! Really, now I have become a human being, a living human being! I am ready to become happy. Let's get down, drink, run, play, see a show. When we are high then let us run along the quiet streets. Go to the beach. I shall stand next to you. I will point my finger like the statue of

Lesseps and say: Bob, this is the Suez Canal; Gateway of the East. Europe lies behind us. We have left behind the civilization which lives on persecution, hatred, revenge and a perpetual desire to win. Now I am entering a new continent. This is the East. It is here that the sun of our happiness is going to dawn again! (p. 61)

But Herta's dream and the dream of some other German Jews to salute the holy land of theirs is not destined to become a reality. 'I am sorry, Sir. German Jews are not allowed on these shores.' This polite but firm reply of the emigration officer shatters the dream. Chakradhar is 'furious, dumbfounded, speechless' and lights his pipe; Herta's impotent fury makes her bite into her own flesh and draw blood (pp. 65f.). She is standing alone on the deck. When Chakradhar finds her there, she touches him to check whether what is happening is reality or another nightmare. 'Why have you come? Only when someone pays attention to you, you realize that you are a human being. But only to be trampled upon again, isn't it?', she asks out of hopeless frustration (p. 66).

While Chakradhar is examining Herta's wound, he notices the ring that she is wearing with KF inscribed on it, and this occasions the narration of Herta's story which Chakradhar tells in his own words. The fourth ten-page-long segment is a hermeneutic achievement of extraordinary quality and one wonders whether any other literary piece written in Marathi at that time even so much as attempted to present such a sensitive picturization of the deadly atmosphere of fear in Fascist Germany and the travails and tribulations of the Jews on the run, let alone do it with such deep feeling. In fact, Chakradhar 'becomes' Herta, his 'other' self, and relives her immediate wretched past. Herta has lost everything—her German boyfriend, her job, her house reduced to ashes, and her senses paralysed. She is in a state of delirium wanting to throw herself in front of the underground train. It is dark. Inadvertently she enters the bathroom at the station and finds herself in front of the big mirror:

She saw her reflection in it. She could not believe it. This five, five-and-a-half feet tall body. Entirely one's own! Such a big treasure it was, she thought. Became conscious of her own existence. Arms, legs, breasts, head—everything got magnified and tried to enter her eyes. You want to destroy all this? How difficult it was! How silly! For a long time she went on looking at herself. Finally went to the tap. Wet her head with water. Came to her senses. Only because she had lost her way had she been saved on that day. (pp. 80f.)

Last day on the ship. News comes that the ship will reach Bombay the following day in the morning and not in the evening as planned. Chakradhar throws his hat into the air and cries: 'Bravo! We'll be home in the morning!' Herta is angry; her hopes are shattered once again. Once again she pulls herself together, prepares for the last night together. They drink, dance, swim together and, at night Herta comes to his cabin, throws her dressing gown violently to the floor and stands naked in front of him like a 'juicy corn-cob emerging out of its sheath':

I know what you are going to say. 'This is not correct. What will people say?' But which people, tell me? Germans, Egyptians or Indians? None of these countries has any place for me. You have a society, people. Their morality. I have been uprooted. I have no people. Which values should I follow, tell me? If you have four walls around you, a house, then you can wear clothes. Cover your shame. But how, and how much, can someone caught in the storm manage to keep himself steady? The violence of the wind, the cruel dance of the waves to go with it. Even the bones rattle. In such a situation, if the clothes on your outer body get torn to shreds, will you still preach morality? (p. 105)

After this emotional and desperate outburst Herta falls unconscious to the floor: 'She was lying like a newly born baby' (p. 109).

*Ranangan*, which had begun as Chakradhar's narrative, ends with Herta's soliloquy presented in the form of three letters of hers to Chakradhar which he translates for the reader. The second letter reveals that Chakradhar had proposed to her which is why Herta interprets the headline in the *Times*: 'Britain is at war with Germany' as the 'epitaph inscribed on the gravestone of our hopes' (p. 111). Apart from describing the desolate state of the mind of Herta and the other Jews on the ship, the letters provide an insight into Herta's changing consciousness which is becoming more and more political, frantically trying to understand the bizarre game life is playing with her:

Bob, till yesterday we all were friends. Today we are enemies! What are we to do? The Nazis say that the Jews are the culprits. The Jews on the ship say that given the opportunity they would join the British army and fight the German Nazis. See, Bob, we Germans want to fight against Germany! Aren't we traitors? Should Germany win or lose? Germany's victory means triumph of the Nazis! Triumph of the philosophy of torture, revenge and strangling of democracy. Germany's defeat means my country's defeat. What should I choose, tell me. Are principles greater or the country? . . . I feel that the narrow bonds of nationalist pride which have spread all over the world should break. . . . My mother comes from Poland; I was born in Berlin. My children will be born in Shanghai. . . . Which country will they fight for? . . . No!

Nazism must not win! Let my country be defeated. . . . And I feel that we women only must fight these war-loving Hitlers! It is our right only! The present civilization has flung the gauntlet at us. Two wars in one generation! Today, the national glory rests on the power to fight, power to destroy, power to kill human beings. The glory of us women rests on the power to create, the power to bear human life! . . . Is it impossible for women to unite those who lose their fathers, brothers, lovers or husbands to the military, and fight against this dictatorship? Bob, if I wanted to fight for the British, will they take me in their army?[13] (pp. 112f.)

This 'helpless woman caught in a calamity' (p. 116) in her last letter expresses her gratitude to Chakradhar for having 'accepted' her soul laden with sorrow, doubt and fear: 'By the sheer look of Jesus the water in the glass turned into a lovely wine!' (p. 117). Her elegy ends with the following line: 'I want you, Bob. But because I can not get you, my soul is torn to pieces' (p. 118)![14]

Although Bedekar calls *Ranangan* 'kalpit' or 'kalpanik'—meaning 'imagined'—his autobiography *Ek Zad Ani Don Pakshi* reveals a different genesis of the text. Bedekar was actually in England at the time. Not for two years but for seven months. The initial euphoria of enjoying a 'free' life disappears quickly because of the threat of war. While being in the thick of that turbulent atmosphere Bedekar becomes introspective: 'In these days he developed a habit—to stroll around all the four sides of each question. To go on circumambulating that question till he had understood it in all its diverse forms.'[15]

Bedekar observed from close quarters the sufferings of about a 150 Jewish refugees on the ship: 'His eardrums almost burst listening to the stories of their torture. He could not bear the burden of that "co-suffering", the mind became numb. . . . This deadly experience was to occasion his novel *Ranangan*.'[16]

Another point which caused him to write *Ranangan* was a matter of personal pride. He wanted to prove to his wife—Balutai, an already established writer—that he, too, could write. At the end of July 1939, Bedekar returned home from abroad and, in August, the novel was there! While pouring on to paper the experiences on the ship, he was constantly asking himself whether it was his autobiography that he was writing or a piece of fiction. He wrote in a frenzy, as if possessed, hiding the text desperately from the eyes of his wife. He could not bear the tension of the first person narrative at times and hence switched over to the third person perspective. He finished it and realized that the flood of sorrow had ebbed. He had been 'freed of his pain'.[17] He dedicates it to a 'Mademoiselle Rolland', meaning his wife.[18] She was influenced by the writing of Romain Rolland, and Bedekar thought that because of the nature of her writing, she could very well be Rolland's adopted daughter. One day, following the publication of *Ranangan*, she praised it and asked Bedekar, whether he had read it. 'No. I wrote it', he answered.[19] So much for the 'fictional' character of *Ranangan*.

It is clear that *Ranangan* functions at several levels. The coincidental meeting of the politically and, therefore, psychologically and emotionally exiled Herta and the psychologically and emotionally deprived Chakradhar can blossom into—even if it is for those ten-eleven days and the way it does—an almost 'divine act of understanding' (*Schleiermacher*) only against an authentically presented 'baroque' experience of Europe on the eve of the Second World War. Both begin to live life as if they were living it for the 'first time'.[20] 'Pathos' is its fulcrum. Both, Chakradhar and Herta 'give up' their respective identities—not because they 'have to' but because they realize that they 'must'. The intensity of understanding their human situation, the horrors of nationalism, its implications in terms of discrimination of various kinds, understanding 'power' and its stranglehold on individual human existences, their communion, is not a causal product of their having 'lost' their identities—the two go together, they are not separate from each other. Bedekar, while responding intensely to the theme of Jewish emigration, succeeds in doing what Milan Kundera expects a novelist to do: 'If the writer considers a historical situation a fresh and revealing possibility of the human world, he will want to describe it as it is. Still, fidelity to historical reality is a secondary matter as regards the value of the novel. The novelist is neither historian nor prophet: he is an explorer of existence.'[21]

In *Ranangan* we have not only the story of the rebirth of Chakradhar and Herta—but also a process of humanization. It is man remembering the 'eclipsed', 'forgotten' and 'concrete' being[22] of his—even if it is only a short-lived glimpse of it that he manages to get.

## NOTES

1. Madhav Achwal, *Rasaswad: Wangmay Ani Kala*. Bombay: Popular Prakashan, 1990 (1st pub. 1962), p. 58.
2. Sarojani Vaidya, 'Udhwasta Parikatha', in *Satyakatha*, May 1969, p. 40.

3. Gangadhar Gadgil, *Sahityache Mandanda*, Bombay: Popular Prakashan, 1990 (1st pub. 1962), p. 234.
4. D.B. Kulkarni, *Tisryanda Ranangan*, Nagpur: Vijay Prakashan, 1976, p. 154.
5. Vasant Tambe, '*Ranangan*: Phadke Paritoshik Milaleli Kadambari', in *Sahyadri*, December-January 1940-1, p. 6.
6. Ibid., p. 7.
7. Kulkarni, op. cit., p. 148. Kulkarni raises the point about the 'universal' character of *Ranangan*: 'Not only is the entire humanity represented on the ship in terms of caste, colour, race and religion, but the various psychological "types" are also present here. The rocking ship on an unsteady, unpredictable sea forms the stage on which we witness—or hear—the timeless cry of the collective human mind.'
8. Achwal, op. cit., p. 58.
9. Vishram Bedekar, *Ranangan,* Pune: Deshmukh Ani Company, 1978 (1st pub. 1939), p. 7. Hereafter there will be only mention of the relevant page number(s) in parantheses referring to this fifth edition of the Marathi text. I am aware that there exists an English translation of *Ranangan*. Unfortunately, however, I do not have access to it and have, therefore, translated the quoted parts of the text myself freely into English. The translation, many times, is intentionally literal, hoping that this may enable the reader to get a taste of the original expression and the 'telegraphic' style. I have translated *Ranangan* into German. Although the translation still awaits publication, the reader, however, can rest assured that I know the text well enough to undertake such an exercise.
10. I am borrowing this concept from Walter Hilsbecher, *Schreiben als Therapie*, Stuttgart: Ernst Klett Verlag, 1967, pp. 9ff. See for a discussion of views of Goethe, Hofmannsthal, Benn, Wittgenstein, Wilhelm Lehmann. Particularly Gottfried Benn's lecture 'Altern als Problem für Künstler' (Aging as a Problem for the Artist) in which he talks about art as 'liberating and relaxing—a cathartic phenomenon'.
11. Vaidya, op. cit., p. 42. Even Vaidya talks in terms of the 'rebirth' of the two main characters and the love between them as the 'first love' in this new life.
12. Roughly translated, the first verses of this German baroque poem written on the background of the Thirty Years' War (1618-48) would read as follows: 'Oh my love, let's hurry We have the time This lingering is a loss Of yours and of mine.'
13. In her foreword to the German translation of *Ranangan* (see note 9) Vidyut Bhagwat discusses the socio-cultural milieu in the Maharashtra of the 1940s. She sees in it already the beginnings of women's lib—thanks to the ever-growing number of educated women—on the one hand, and the emergence of an anti-Brahmanical sentiment, which was

a product of various reformist movements, on the other. These two factors not only encouraged a greater understanding of the relationship between the 'Self and the Other' within one's own immediate context, but also created the necessary ground for 'making one's own' the 'Jewish condition'.

14. Here it may not be out of place to quote a spontaneous reaction of an average Marathi reader while reading this strange 'foreign' text. Tambe, while pointing out the significance of *Ranangan* for the 'thinking youth', formulates it as follows: 'While reading it you feel—this is the real world around us, with its conflicts, differences and also its vastness. This is not a make-belief [*sic*] world, creation of a puppet theatre. While he goes on reading it, the reader says to himself: "Why did writers never tell me all this before? I am coming to know of all these happenings in the world so late. Also I am realizing only now that a writer can tell you such important things!"' (p. 8).
15. Vishram Bedekar, *Ek Zad Ani Don Pakshi,* Bombay: Popular Prakashan, 1984, p. 154. Even the autobiography is a third person narrative. At the beginning of the text there is a quote from the *Mundakopanishad*: 'That there are two birds on the tree of life. Living in friendship. One of them eats the fruit. The other eats nothing. He merely observes. The first one is powerless despite eating the fruit. The other is powerful in spite of remaining hungry.' The narrator of the (auto)biography is this second bird—technique which dominates *Ranangan* . All quotes from the Marathi original translated by me.
16. Ibid., p. 155.
17. Ibid., p. 163. The tone reminds one of Kafka's *Tagebücher* (Diaries) or his *Letters to Felice*. See Bruno Hillebrand. *Theorie des Romans*, München: Deutscher Taschenbuch Verlag, 1980 (1st pub. 1972), p. 316. The theme is the same: writing as a process of self-liberation.
18. Ibid., p. 164. The critics quoted in this text were obviously not aware of this fact, since *Ek Zad Ani Don Pakshi* was written and published much later.
19. Ibid., p. 164. The book then, at the behest of Bedekar, did not carry the name of the author.
20. Victor Cp. Sklovskij, *Theorie der Prosa*. Edited and translated from the Russian by Gisela Drohla. Frankfurt/Main: S. Fischer Verlag , 1966 (1st pub. 1925).
21. Milan Kundera, *The Art of the Novel.* Translated by Linda Asher, Rupa Paperback, 1992 (1st pub. 1986, English transl. 1988), p. 44.
22. Ibid., pp. 3f.

# To Rudolf von Leyden: A Letter out of Season

*Krishen Khanna*

A 1/51 Panchsheel Enclave
New Delhi 110001, Tel: 6461132

Rudi,

It was you who did the writing while we waited to see what you had to say about us in your columns. In the early 1950s hardly any art was sold. Even your critical approval didn't do much to convince people to buy, though they all came with approving and disapproving faces. None of us even expected economic benefits to flow from your pen. What we received and valued was your critical appraisal which was tense and frank but never brutal. You were only writing the truth when you once commented on my poor drawing. I never told you this but for four years after your comment, I abandoned all colour and worked at what was weakest in my pictorial vocabulary. I must have produced dozens of paintings in umbers and blacks. Years later you commented on the strength of my drawing little realizing why and how it had happened.

Most unfortunate were the events which brought you to Bombay, but our gain was incalculable. The timing seems in retrospect to have been just right. Souza, Raza and Ara had formed the Progressive Artists Group. It provoked hostility but, at the same time, it attracted artists with modernist inclinations. Your encouragement and espousal of the works of these artists fortified their position. The academicians of the Art School perceived a threat in modernity and the dean forbade its staff and students to have anything to do with these artists. Even now at this hopelessly late stage, there are murmurs of the damage done by 'Western' ideas. Now, some 40 or more years later, when the apparent modernity of art has become commonplace, it is difficult to imagine the initial resistance to it. I sometimes wonder what you would have thought of the current proliferation of what passes as modern art. 'It's academic' you would say. Academism, far from denoting a particular style, was an attitude of mind for you. When a style congealed into a mannerism and became impervious to change, it spelt death. You celebrated the forces of life whenever you found them, in ancient art or modern, in Europe or in Asia. The term 'globalism' which is so current now, had not been invented in your day.

No one can forget the formidable defence you put up in the case of obscenity against Akbar Padamsee who had shown an innocuous painting entitled 'Lovers'. You placed the court in a most awkward position by producing photographs of Khajuraho and Konarak. It was put in the most embarrassing position of either sending Akbar to jail and denouncing our 'Ancient Indian heritage', or accepting Akbar's painting as a valuable addition to that heritage. Akbar won out, so did you and all of us. It has become case law now, which means it is forgotten and can only surface when someone in the same or similar predicament goes to the courts again. Them as in power now still use repression. Rushdie's *The Moor's Last Sigh* is under a blackout here. We haven't quite got to the public destruction of books but have developed far more insidious means of gagging. You would have recognized the scent. I suppose this tussle will be never ending and visions of an egalitarian and a wise and just society are Utopian dreams of the naive. Depressing thoughts indeed which are apt to paralyse creativity?

Maybe one should also concern oneself with beautiful objects and weave in and out of works of great craftsmanship which we rightly or wrongly believe will endure even our troubled times. You certainly had passions which I couldn't quite understand at first. For instance, your great love for Ganjifa playing cards. Beautiful they surely were and your collection, made with such patience and expense, was probably one of the best in the world. You were not only satisfied at building and owning the collection, you went on to learn the many games which were played throughout this country. I bet you too could play a crafty hand. You lectured on the subject and became a prominent member of Ganjifa Societies in Europe and held meetings of delegates from all over Europe. It amused me as much as it baffled me till I realized that I was guilty of trying to make you conform to a one-dimensional image, that of a standard bearer of modern Indian art.

Gradually and over a period of time and in many places—Bombay (now reverted to as Mumbai), Madras (Chennai), Delhi, Shimla, Bhopal and Vienna, your other interests unfolded. Mangoes! and how you loved them. I almost came to believe that gorging on these was a prime passion and even thought that your annual visits, always coinciding with the mango season, were to quench your lust for what you said was the most noble of fruits. Your wanderlust was something everybody knew about. You thought nothing of going to the most inaccessible of places to see an old sculpture or a disused and ruined temple. Sleeping under an open sky and eating what the local population would provide with relish. My grandmother who had performed every pilgrimage which a good Hindu is expected to make, couldn't match your score. You seemed to take it all so blithely. 'While Lolly and I were trekking in Kashmir, we spent a day climbing Hara Kukh' as if that was some little hillock on your way. So when I expressed my surprise at your prowess for climbing, you came out with a long list of places which you said you had to traverse as a part of your doctorate in geology. My goodness, I'd always thought you had a doctorate in art history.

Do you wonder at my surprise when you told me that you were going to settle in Paris on retirement from Voltas? I had the cheek to tell you that you wouldn't be happy. After all, what had really mattered to you was right here in the country which had adopted you. True, you might not have a mansion to live in and you wouldn't be an official *burra sahib* but you could have a *barsati* and a host of friends who would never abandon you. Your circumstances were such as to leave you no choice. You went and I am sorry I was right. I could never see you as a Parisian. The informality and ease to which you'd become accustomed was not to be found again. Your enthusiasms for Ganjifa, for modern or ancient Indian art found few takers and you were never one who found solace in anonymity. Sadly and happily, you had to leave Paris and move to Vienna, that 'city of a Million Melodies' as the song would have it. Even there you found the entrée difficult. Established and ancient cultures are wary and self-preserving. I found it difficult not to smile when you told me that the 'von' before your surname was a great asset in Vienna. So they have a caste system too, I thought. You were at an age when it's altogether more comfortable and convenient to go along than to do battle on a new soil.

You cultivated the biggest and brightest begonias I've ever seen, tended a lawn which skirted the Vienna woods and made friends with kindly neighbours. What a changed scenario I thought. Of course you were lonely though you wouldn't admit it. You couldn't fool me with all that scurrying around and gathering Ganjifa enthusiasts who would arrive with their secret knowledge of the game and probably muttered 'no bid'.

Seeing you leading this somewhat solitary existence, I asked you what would happen if you took ill. You guessed what was on my mind and pointed to the neighbours next door. 'They look in frequently', you said. Yet when the Angel announced his entry, there was no one. You had realized as much. With your usual efficiency and eye to detail, you bade the Angel wait, called up the medical emergency, donned on your greatcoat, your muffler, your fur cap, your gloves, kept the door open and sat down beside the telephone and waited. That's where they found you, all ready for your journey. They tried but couldn't bring you back.

Someone called me the next morning, I think it was Lolly and I felt the last lines of *The Exile's Letter* which you so loved:

And if you ask how I regret that parting
It was like the flowers falling at Spring's end
Confused, whirled in a tangle.

And now the things and people you so loved are scattered and you rest with your ancestors in Partenkirchen.

*Au revoir* dear friend, may we recognize each other, even in our different shapes, in our future lives and continue where we had left.

Krishen

"WHAT A CRIME TO
DESTROY OUR KULTUR"

DENLEY

RUHR

JUNK!

Picture by Rudolf von Leyden.

# Contributors

ANIL BHATTI

Is Professor of German at the Centre of German Studies, Jawaharlal Nehru University, New Delhi. He joined the faculty of the Centre in 1971 after completing his doctorate in *Germanistik* from the University of Munich. He was fellow of the Alexander von Humboldt Foundation 1975-6, 1981-2 at the University of Bielefeld and has been member of the visiting faculty of the Universities of Kassel and Goettingen. His current area of research concerns problems of literature, colonialism and Orientalism with special reference to Germany and India.

RAJENDRA DENGLE

Was born in 1956 in Bombay. He attended Marathi and English medium schools in Pune and completed his studies at Poona University as a Bachelor of Arts in philosophy in 1976 and in German in 1977. At the Jawaharlal Nehru University (JNU) in New Delhi, he did his M.A. in German literature, concluding his research work there with a Ph.D. thesis on Ödön von Horvath in 1990. He is now working as an Associate Professor at the Centre of German Studies at the JNU, teaching subjects such as theories of literature and history of literature. His present fields of research include Fritz Mauthner and the literature of *fin de siècle*, translation of German literary texts into Marathi and vice versa, and also theatre and painting.

MARTIN KÄMPCHEN

Was born in 1948 in Boppard, Germany. He received his early education in his home-town, and studied at Vienna and Paris. His subjects included German literature, philosophy, theatre and French. He received his Ph.D. in German literature from Vienna University. Since 1973 he has been living in India. After teaching German at

Calcutta, he returned to comparative religion at Madras University and Santiniketan, completing his work with a Ph.D. He is presently translating Ramakrishna's and Tagore's writings from Bengali into German. Besides that, he writes and edits books on Indian religions and interreligious and intercultural dialogue. The writing of fiction is another line of his manifold activities.

REKHA KAMATH

Was born in 1953 in New Delhi. After completing an M.A. in German Literature from the Jawaharlal Nehru University in 1972, she joined the faculty of the Centre of German Studies, JNU, where she is now a Professor of German literature. She has worked on the presentation of alterity in German literature and is currently working on German missionaries in India. She was a fellow of the Alexander von Humboldt Foundation at the Free University, Berlin, 1990-1.

KRISHEN KHANNA

Was born in 1925 in Lyallpur, Punjab. He studied at the Imperial Services College, Windsor, UK, 1938-42, at Emerson College, Multan in 1942, and at the Government College, Lahore, 1943-4, completing his studies with a B.A. (Hons) in English literature. In 1948, he joined Grindlays Bank as a covenanted officer, resigning in 1961 to devote his full time to art. In 1962-3 he was Fellow of the Rockefeller Council of Economic and Cultural Affairs, and in 1963-4 Artist in Residence at the American University, Washington, DC. His works were exhibited in Bombay, Madras, Calcutta, Delhi, Tokyo, Washington, DC, London, New York and are represented in many private and public collections, notably at the National Gallery of Modern Art, New Delhi; the Museum of Modern Art, New York; the Contemporary Art Society, London; Glenbana Art Museum, Japan; and Lalit Kala Akademi, New Delhi. He was awarded the Gold Medal of the 1st Triennale in India; the 1st Biennale in Pakistan; the President's award at Baghdad. The President of India conferred on him the Padma Shri. He has been serving as adviser to various institutions, including the Government of India, Ministry of Culture; the Jawaharlal Nehru Fund; and as Chairman, purchasing committee, National Gallery of Modern Art, New Delhi. He was member of the General Council, Executive Committee, Executive Board and Finance Committee of the Lalit Kala Akademi, New Delhi. He lectured on art at the JNU, New Delhi; at Berkeley University, California; and delivered the annual Gandhi Memorial Lecture at the Raman Research Institute, Bangalore, in 1990.

RAINER LOTZ

Was born in 1953 in Wertheim, Baden-Württemberg. He completed his studies in *Germanistik,* sociology, history and Hindi at the University of Heidelberg with an M.A. in 1979. He was a DAAD-lecturer at the JNU from 1986 to 1992. In cooperation with SFB 309 (special research programme, financed by the German Research Council) 'Die Literarische Übersetzung' (Literary Translation) at the University of Goettingen and the Centre of German Studies at the JNU, he did his Ph.D. on the translation and reception of Bertold Brecht's poetry in modern Hindi. Besides teaching assignments at various Indian universities and research in the field of translation studies, intercultural hermeneutics and comparative studies of literature, he is presently engaged in translation projects between Indian and European languages.

JOACHIM OESTERHELD

Was born in Hartha, Sachsen. Studying ethnology as well as history and languages of South-East Asia at the Humboldt University in Berlin, he graduated with 'Diplom' in 1967. After joining the Institute for International Relations in Potsdam-Babelsberg and staying in India from 1973 to 1978, he did his Dr.rer.pol. in 1981. From then onwards till 1997 he was with the Institute for Asian and African Sciences at the Humboldt University ('Habilitation' in 1989). He is at present Fellow at the Centre for Modern Oriental Studies in Berlin. Actively involved in teaching and research he has been working on contemporary Indian history and politics and the history of German-Indian relations.

TILAK RAJ SAREEN

Was born in Lahore in 1935. He studied at the Punjab University, Chandigarh, where he did his Ph.D. In 1958 he joined the National Archives of India, and was appointed associate editor of the 'Towards Freedom Project' in 1984. He served with the Indian Institute of Public Administration in 1963-5, was record management consultant with the Government of Kenya 1980-1, was Visiting Fellow at the University of Heidelberg in 1993 and the University of Tokyo 1994-5. From 1985 to 1996 he served as director/member secretary of the Indian Council of Historical Research. Having retired he was reappointed as consultant in 1996. He is working at present on 'India and the Japanese Occupation of South-East Asia during the Second World War'.

AGATA SCHINDLER

Was born in 1947 in Levoca, Czechoslovakia. She studied piano at the Conservatory in Kosice, and musicology at the University of Bratislava, concluding her studies there with a doctorate in 1984. She has been working for 20 years as a journalist mainly for Slovakian and Czech specialist publications, for publishing houses specialized in music and for the radio. Since 1981 she has been living in Dresden. From 1981 to 1990 she was Secretary of the Society of Composers and Musicologists in the District of Dresden. From 1995 to 1997 she participated in establishing the Research and Information Centre for Outlawed Music at the Dresden Centre for Contemporary Music. She has recently done research on Walter Kaufmann and other ostracized musicians. She read and published papers in Germany, India, the Czechian Republic and Slovakia.

MAJID HAYAT SIDDIQI

Is a Professor of contemporary history, at the Centre for Historical Studies, JNU. He has researched and published studies in agrarian history and peasant oral tradition in the colonial period, and is currently working on mentality histories in early Indian nationalism. His school and university education has been in India. Over the years he has been Agatha Harrison Fellow at the University of Oxford (1976-8), Visiting Fulbright Fellow at the University of Chicago (1986) and Senior Visiting Fellow at the International Institute for Asian Studies, Leiden (1997).

JOHANNES H. VOIGT

Was born in 1929 in Gross-Wittensee, Schleswig-Holstein. Studying law, history and English at the Universities of Kiel, Marburg, London and Oxford, he completed his studies with 'Staatsexamen' and D.Phil.

at Kiel and D.Phil. at Oxford. During 1959-61 he was lecturer in German at the Benares Hindu University, Varanasi, and 1961-2 in history at the Panjab University, Chandigarh. After research work in London, Oxford, New Delhi, he became Research Fellow at the Australian National University, Canberra. In 1973 he was appointed *Dozent* after his 'Habilitation' at Stuttgart University. He became professor there in 1978. He retired from teaching in 1995 and is at present working on relations between Germany and India since the Second World War.

SHALVA WEIL

Was born in London and graduated from the London School of Economics in sociology in 1971. In 1972, she received her M.A. in multiracial studies from Sussex University, England, and wrote a dissertation on Bene Israel Indian Jews in Britain. In 1977, she received a D.Phil. degree in anthropology, after completing a thesis on the 'Persistence of Ethnicity among Bene Israel Indian Jews in the town of Lod, Israel', based on three years' fieldwork among the community. She has been resident in Israel since the 1970s, where she is senior lecturer in the department of Education at Ben-Gurion University of the Negev and senior researcher at the NCJW Research Institute for Innovation in Education at the Hebrew University of Jerusalem. She has edited a book on Cochin Jewry (in Hebrew) and published a large number of academic articles on the subject of Indian Jewry in India and in Israel. In 1995, she was appointed the general editor of the World Heritage Press Hindu-Judaic Studies Series and is a member of several Indian scientific journals' editorial boards. She is the chairperson of the Israel-India Cultural Association.

Manohar

M-114

13/5/99